THE
LITANY OF LORETO

THE

LITANY OF LORETO

By RICHARD KLAVER, O.S.C.

B. Herder Book Co.
15 & 17 SOUTH BROADWAY, ST. LOUIS 2, MO.
and 33 QUEEN SQUARE, LONDON, W.C.

IMPRIMI POTEST

Lawrence J. Kerich, O.S.C.
Vicar General

NIHIL OBSTAT

Francis P. Pitka, O.S.C.
Censor Deputatus

IMPRIMATUR

✠ John Francis Noll, D.D.
Archbishop-Bishop of
Fort Wayne

March 12, 1954

FOREWORD

In the attempt to write a doctrinal treatise about Our Lady, one is confronted with the necessity of making a choice among the several methods which may be employed to sing the praises of Mary. To view Mary's position in close relationship with the doctrine of redemption and grace, would mean to treat it as a part of dogmatic theology. To develop the revealed facts about Mary in their positive and speculative aspects, and arrange them into a systematic unit which shows vital connection with the organic whole of dogmatic truths, would mean an ex professo Mariology. One may consider the work at hand as a devotional task and endeavor to show the interdependence of Marian lore and ascetical theology; even use it as a medium to emphasize the mystical aspect. All these methods are effective and show definite merits.

To use the Litany of Loreto with its great variety of invocations as framework, while trying to maintain throughout a continuity of thought and doctrine, is not devoid of manifold complications. It furnishes, however, an opportunity to combine the theological point of view with the devotional, while retaining a uniformity which is based on the original structure of the Litany in its historical development. In this manner, the author aimed to present the reader with a more or less complete Mariology in a novel guise. It is his sincere hope that he has completed the task with some semblance of success.

The doctrine presented in this volume is not original. I have endeavored to give what is most commonly held by theologians, especially those of the Thomistic school. For the positive part of this book, besides giving due prominence to Sacred Scripture and patristic literature, I have made extensive use of the comprehensive writings of Fathers Scheeben and Garrigou-Lagrange, thus assuring myself and the reader of a foundation which is at once scholarly and inspired by a deep devotion to Our Blessed Lady.

Quotations from the Old Testament follow the Douay version. New Testament texts are from the official translation of the Confraternity of Christian Doctrine (Copyright 1941).

Francis J. Connell, C.SS.R., Dean of the Faculty of Theology at the Catholic University of Washington, D.C., has allowed us to quote from an article published in *Our Lady's Digest*. The same magazine and its editor, Father Stanley Matuszewski, M.S., permitted us to use several quotations from the writings of Jacques Maritain, Don Sharkey, and Father Cooney. *The Field Afar* permitted us to cite the experiences of Fathers Madigan and McCabe. The Montfort Fathers of Bay Shore, N.Y., granted the use of St. Louis de Montfort's book, *True Devotion to the Blessed Virgin*. We are grateful to the Paulist Fathers for permission to use quotations from the book, *Sermons and Conferences of John Tauler, O.P.* The *N.C.W.C. News Service*, Washington, D.C., allowed us to relate the story of Father Florentine Castanon. Time magazine permitted us to quote from the *Diary of a Rumanian Priest* (Copyright 1951).

We express our sincere gratitude to the above publishers and authors.

Our Lady of the Lake Seminary
Wawasee, Indiana

CONTENTS

x CONTENTS

CHAPTER 1

THE LITANY OF LORETO

As an established form of divine worship, the litany is a prayer of responsive petition. With its repetition of an identical refrain, it constitutes a vocal prayer which is at once adapted to common purpose, and it has proved eminently useful to implore God's aid for averting public calamities, or to obtain guidance in private necessities. Its form is modeled after Biblical examples of public prayers which, accompanied by musical instruments, were chanted in unison. The following is an illustration, taken from the Book of Psalms.

"Praise the Lord, for He is good:
    for His mercy endureth forever.
Praise the God of gods:
    for His mercy endureth forever.
Praise the Lord of lords:
    for His mercy endureth forever" (Ps. 135);

and thus through its twenty-seven strophes, with the identical concluding eulogium for each verse.

Prayers in litany form are frequently used in the Mass-liturgy of the Oriental Church. Toward the end of the first part of Mass, the deacon, who formulates the petitions, invites the catechumens to join in common prayer. After the departure of the catechumens, he summons the baptized congregation to pray in like manner for the peace and welfare of the world, for the Holy, Catholic, and Apostolic Church, and for several related intentions. After each petition the congregation responds with *Kyrie Eleison,* until the concluding impetrations, to which they answer "Deliver us, O Lord," and "We beseech Thee hear us." Here we find a striking resemblance to the last petitions of our Litany of the Saints. The frequent repetition of the *Kyrie Eleison* was probably the original form of the litany. We find a trace of it in the Mass, where the triple repetition of the *Kyrie* and *Christe Eleison* seems to point to former litany prayers which, at a very early time, formed an integral part of the Roman Mass-liturgy. In the Ambrosian rite of the Mass, two litanies are recited on Sundays of Lent instead of the Gloria. The Roman rite still calls for a full litany on the feast of St. Mark, on Rogation days, during the liturgical ceremonies of Holy Saturday, and on the Saturday before Pentecost. It also forms a part of the Ordination Mass, and is used when a bishop or a church is consecrated.

When the Church emerged from the Catacombs, public devotions became common and processions were held frequently. The custom was most general in Rome, particularly during Lent. Pope, clergy, and faithful, while chanting litanies, would go in procession to a different church each day, in order to celebrate the Sacred Mysteries of Holy Mass. Such processions became known as litanies. Thus originated the Major Litany, which was held on the 25th day of April to replace the pagan festival of Robigalia, on which day the Romans held processions and supplications to their gods. The Minor Litany of the Rogation days before Ascension was introduced by St. Mamertus, Bishop of Vienne, on account of the earthquakes then prevalent (477).

The Fifth Council of Orleans (511) prescribed the Rogation days in their existing form, for the whole of Gaul, while Leo III approved them for Rome, in 799. From there they spread throughout the universal Church.

The litany, popularized through its use in processions and Mass-liturgy, soon appeared in numberless variations, especially during the Middle Ages. In his Ecclesiastical Annals, Cardinal Baronius mentions about eighty forms then extant, which honored God the Father, the Son, the Holy Spirit, the Precious Blood, the Blessed Virgin, and various saints. In order to prevent abuse, Clement VIII, by decree of the Inquisition of Sept. 6, 1601, forbade the publication of any litany, except that of the saints and the Litany of Loreto, unless approved by the Congregation of Rites. At present, the Litany of the Sacred Heart, of the Holy Name of Jesus, of All Saints, and of St. Joseph, together with the Litany of Loreto enjoy approval for public use.

The text of the Litany of Loreto, as we have it today, is composed after the plan of several Marian litanies of earlier date. It had the good fortune to be adopted in the famous shrine of Loreto, and found its way from there into other countries. Its formal approval for use in the universal Church dates from 1587.

As a processional prayer, particularly to avert public calamities, the Litany of Loreto began to replace the Litany of the Saints probably during the fifteenth century, for in the following century we find it prescribed for penitential processions "as being in accordance with ancient custom." Cardinal Francis Toledo introduced it into the Basilica of S. Maria Maggiore in 1597; and Pope Paul V ordered it to be sung in that Church, morning and evening, on Saturdays and on vigils and feasts of the Madonna (1613). As a result of this example, the Loreto Litany was generally adopted and is today the only Marian litany approved everywhere, for both private and public devotion.

CHAPTER 2

THE HOLY NAME OF MARY

Before we attempt to give an explanation of the various invocations of the Litany of Our Lady, we must try to establish the etymology of the name Mary. This is no easy task, since well over seventy interpretations of Mary's name are found in the works of different authors.

The name Maria or Mariam, as found in the Greek version of the New Testament, undoubtedly represents the Hebrew name *Miriam*. In the Old Testament it appears only once as the name of the sister of Moses and Aaron, who all three were born in Egypt. As such, it does not exclude the possibility that the name Mary is of Egyptian origin. The name Moses is definitely Egyptian, and was given him by the daughter of Pharaoh, "because," she said, "I took him out of the water" (Exod. 2:10). Nor does the name Aaron find its counterpart in the Hebrew language. In case the name Mary is of Egyptian derivation, it means "the beloved one," and is most suitable for an only daughter, such as Mary was. But why should the name Mary have been chosen by the parents of Our Blessed Lady, or by a number of others mentioned in the New Testament, if the name were Egyptian?

Considering a Hebrew origin, the name *Miriam* may be

derived either from "Marah," which means to be rebel-
lious, or from "Mara," which means to be well nourished.
Etymology does not decide which of these two is to be pre-
ferred. But it seems hardly probable that the name of a
young girl should be connected with the idea of rebellion,
unless there is a mystical meaning to be added in the case of
the Blessed Virgin, in accordance with the text of the Protevangelium: "I will put enmities between thee and the
woman, and thy seed and her seed: she shall crush thy head,
and thou shalt lie in wait for her heel" (Gen. 3:15). That
such a mystical interpretation could be inferred seems feas-
ible from the entire analogy of revelation. The Fathers also
attach a mystical meaning to the traditional names of
Mary's parents. Joachim means "preparation of the Lord";
and the name of Anna means "grace." Our Lord Himself
bore the name Jesus by divine revelation, "for He shall
save His people from their sins" (Matt. 1:21). Is it too
much to expect that the name Mary should likewise possess
a meaning by virtue of divine inspiration, which corresponds to the dignity and position of her who bears it? It
seems at least improbable that God, who conceived from
all eternity the exalted state of Mary as the Mother of God
in all possible details, should have left this detail to chance.

Assuming that the name of Mary was specifically willed
by God, we may now turn to the other given stem of the
Hebrew name, which is "Mara," and signifies to be well
nourished. In view of the fact that Orientals consider the
idea of being well nourished as synonymous with beauty
and bodily perfection, it is a name apt to be given to any
young girl. In the case of Mary it would mean "the beautiful," or "the perfect one." But searching deeper Mary's
name may readily point at her fullness of grace. The Fathers explain the words with which the Angel addressed

Mary, "Hail, full of grace," as expressive of a distinguishing mark of her person. Thus, "full of Grace" is Mary's proper name, much in the same way as Eve was called "Mother of All the Living" (Gen. 3:20), or as our Lord was named Christ, the Anointed.

The Holy Name of Mary has been cherished in the Church as a precious possession from early apostolic times. Both Fathers and spiritual writers of later ages, have been full of praise in reference to this Holy Name. St. Bonaventure declares that the name of Mary cannot be pronounced without bringing some grace to him who does so devoutly. Thomas à Kempis affirms that the devils fear the Queen of heaven to such a degree, that only hearing her name pronounced makes them fly from him who does so as from a burning fire. "Thy Holy Name, O Mary," says St. Ambrose, "is a precious ointment, which breathes forth the odor of divine grace." And St. Bernard advises: "In dangers, in perplexities, in every doubt, think of Mary, call on Mary: let her name not leave thy lips, let her not depart from thy heart."

A special day has been assigned by the Church to honor Mary's name. The feast was first observed at Cuenca in Spain, in 1513. It spread in that country, and in 1671 was granted to all its dioceses, as well as to the Kingdom of Naples. In 1683, Pope Innocent XI extended it to the whole Western Church, as an act of thanksgiving for the raising of the siege of Vienna and the defeat of the Turks by John Sobieski. At that time it was assigned to the Sunday within the octave of Our Lady's birthday. It is now kept on Sept. 12, the day of Sobieski's triumph.

CHAPTER 3

HOLY MOTHER OF GOD

Mary's first glorious title is that of Mother of God. The divine maternity is the first of many honors which came to Mary, and its import is such that all the titles which follow pertain to Mary because of this one, which holds in embryo all that can be said to honor her.

Sacred Scripture nowhere employs the formal expression, Mother of God. But apart from the explicit revelations concerning the being and origin of Christ, Sacred Scripture contains all the elements of Mary's divine maternity as included therein. We have but to refer to the prophecy of Isaias, which reads: "Behold a virgin shall conceive, and bear a Son, and His name shall be called Emmanuel" (Is. 7:14). This was further explained by the Angel. "The Holy Spirit shall come upon thee and the power of the Most High shall overshadow thee; and therefore the Holy One to be born shall be called the Son of God" (Luke 1:35). In addition, we have the salutation of Elizabeth: "Blessed art thou among women and blessed is the fruit of thy womb! And how have I deserved that the Mother of my Lord should come to me?" (Luke 1:42–43)

It cannot be said, as the Nestorians did, that the Blessed Mother simply brought forth the human nature of Christ, as a person indeed, but not as a divine Person. By representing the human nature as a complete man, and the Incarnation as the assumption of a man by the divine Word, the Nestorians denied the human birth and the sonship of the divine Word, precisely because they denied the identity of the person of Christ with the Second Person of the Holy Trinity. The Catholic dogma, however, is very explicit. The first canon of the Council of Ephesus (431) declares: "If one does not profess: that God is the true Emmanuel, and that consequently the Holy Virgin is the Mother of God: for she brought forth according to the flesh the Word of God, which became flesh, let him be anathema." And again, the sixth canon of the Fifth Ecumenical Council (553): "If one attests that the holy and ever glorious Virgin Mary is only in a sense, and not really, the Mother of God, let him be anathema." Likewise the third canon of the Council of Lateran (649): "If anyone does not profess that Mary is truly and appropriately the holy Mother of God, inasmuch as, in the fullness of time, she conceived of the Holy Spirit, without seed, the very Word of God, and brought forth Him who was born of the Father from all eternity, let him be anathema."

According to the explicit wording of the dogma, it can and must be said that the Word Incarnate is the material product of Mary: that is to say, the Second Person of the Most Holy Trinity was conceived by Mary and born of her. She brought forth the complete Christ, even as natural or human motherhood has essential reference to a compound, personal being, consisting of body and soul. The mother's activity extends itself to the material product, which is the body, while the soul is infused by God directly. Yet the mother is the mother not of the mere body but of the human person, which consists of the body in connection with the life-giving soul. It may truly be said that the full personality of the child receives existence in consequence of this production and, even though the natural production does not bring forth the soul, still the soul is created by God and instilled into the body on account of, and in consequence of the natural producing activity of the mother. In an analogous manner, the relation of the divine motherhood in Mary refers directly and formally to the divine Person of the Word of God, inasmuch as the divine Word assumed His flesh of her and in her. It would be wrong to say that Mary had a part in the eternal and spiritual origin of the Word. But it would be equally wrong to represent the maternal cooperation of Mary as if, by itself, it were directed merely to the bringing about of the human nature of Christ. Since the human and the divine in Christ are united inseparably by the hypostatic union, Mary is the mother of Him who is the Word Incarnate, conceived and produced in her under the supernatural influence of God. In other words: while the pure Divinity was strictly born of the Father, the same incarnate Divinity was strictly born of Mary. In addition we may say that, from a natural point of view, the child is to the mother something which is given her by God, which she clothed with her flesh, or to which she communicated and appropriated her flesh, and with which she herself is connected through this communication. In like manner, Jesus, the Blessed Fruit of Mary's womb, is first and foremost a gift of God to His Mother, according to the word of the Angel: "The Holy One to be born of thee" (Luke 1:35). But, precisely where motherhood is taken as a personal relation between mother and child, the producing activity of the mother finds its ultimate term in the higher origin of the child. Thus, the mother exists because of the child, rather than that the child exists because of the mother.

Under this aspect, Jesus is the Child of promise, who was destined "for the fall and the rise of many in Israel" (Luke 2:34).

In considering Mary's glorious title of Mother of God, no one needs to fear that the honor of God and of Christ is infringed by the stressing of her divine maternity. On the other hand, grave danger threatens the honor of Christ, if His Mother is not gladly and emphatically proclaimed the Mother of God. As the Nestorians opposed this title because they did not acknowledge Christ as true God, so Protestantism has slowly lost the full knowledge of the divinity of Christ because it refuses Mary the honor which is due her as the Mother of God. We must forever view Mary in the light of her Son, as we must study her privileges as an organic whole in the work of salvation; for to separate Christ from His Mother is to divide Christ. Through the long history of the Church, it has been the sad experience of those who rejected Mary and failed to give her full honor as the true Mother of God, that they lost Christ as well, for the Child will not be separated from His mother.

CHAPTER 4

HOLY VIRGIN OF VIRGINS

When the Church addresses Mary not merely as Virgin but as Virgin of Virgins, she wishes to express the absolute, perfect virginity of the Mother of God. Virginity, in its moral aspect, is the purpose of mind to preserve perfect chastity by abstaining from sexual pleasure, whether from the lawful use of marriage or from lust. Physically it implies a bodily integrity, visible evidence of which exists in women only. It implies a material element, which establishes the fact of its presence in the past and in the present; and a formal element, which includes a firm purpose to retain it in the future. In this chapter we intend to treat of only one phase of Mary's perfect virginity, the mystery of her virginal conception, leaving the treatment of the other aspects to later chapters.

Like the divine maternity of Our Lady, the virginal conception was foretold by the prophet with the words: "The Lord Himself shall give you a sign. Behold a virgin shall conceive, and bear a son, and his name shall be Emmanuel" (Is. 7:14). That the strength of this prophecy lies in the virgin who shall conceive and bear a son is evident from the context. There would be no question of a sign or miracle, unless these words point to a virginal conception. Mary no doubt knew this prophecy, and was conscious of the fact that the Messiah was to be born of a virgin. But when Gabriel appeared to her in her humble home of Nazareth, revealing that she would conceive and bear a son, who would be great and be called the Son of the Most High, there remained a possibility that the Angel was speaking of someone other than the promised Emmanuel. Thus she prudently inquired how this would be accomplished, since she had firmly resolved to remain a virgin. The subsequent explanation of the Angel, "The Holy Spirit shall come upon thee and the power of the Most High shall overshadow thee," gave her a complete solution of the question of her virginity, while the accompanying words, "The Holy One to be born shall be called the Son of God" (Luke 1:35), removed the final doubt of her selection to become the mother of the Messiah. It was at that moment that she spoke her words of acceptance which brought the Eternal Word of God into her womb: and the Word was made flesh to dwell among men.

When the Apostles Creed states that our Lord was conceived of the Holy Spirit, it definitely precludes the influence of a human, material element to effect Mary's conception. On the other hand it establishes a supernatural influence of a spiritual and divine principle working upon Mary in a purely preternatural manner. Nor did this unusual way, which brought fertility to the fruit of her womb, cause any detriment to the reality of the complete female production, since divine power simply provided in a direct manner, and in a miraculous way, the productive principle which God otherwise provides indirectly, and by means of the impregnating influence of man.

In order to understand the virginal conception, in connection with the dogma of the motherhood of Mary, it is important that we measure the specific activity of all maternal production. The natural activity of the mother before conception includes the formation of the organic seed, susceptible of impregnation. Upon impregnation, it becomes a living fruit. Thereupon the natural activity of the mother consists in the further formation and development of the fruit, thereby enabling it to live independently and apart from the mother, at the completion of which process it is brought into the world. The determining principle in natural production is the paternal influence. The essential office of the mother is one of simple cooperation with this paternal principle, upon which in reality the existence of the living fruit depends. The mother's productive activity is one of preparing and forming the body, and thus providing the material being or substance of the child. But she does not directly contribute to his existence as a person, for which the paternal principle is at once necessary and sufficient. In the case of Mary, the paternal principle was directly provided by divine omnipotence, for which reason God Himself is the true Father of Jesus Christ in the external production of the divine Word. Mary of course provided complete maternal activity such as every natural mother provides in the generation of her son, and thus she merits the name of mother of our Savior in the full sense of the word.

The supernatural and purely spiritual process of bringing forth the Savior of the world was indeed so fitting that the natural way would have been inappropriate. St. Thomas proposes four reasons which illustrate the appropriateness of the virginal conception.

The first reason is bound up with the dignity of the Father who sent the Son, according to the word of St. Paul: "When the fullness of time came, God sent His Son, born of a woman" (Gal. 4:4). Since Christ is the true and the natural Son of God, it would not have been proper that He would have a father other than God alone, lest the dignity of God, as Father, would have to be transferred to a human being, and Christ would stand in a relation of essential dependence to a creature.

The second reason redounds to the dignity of the Son who was sent, He Himself being God. The divine Word was conceived by the Father from all eternity in the most complete purity of spirit. Since the flesh was assumed by the Word of God in order to make it the flesh of the divine Word, it was proper that this flesh also should be conceived in the most complete purity of the mother. In other words, Christ's temporal production by the mother could not be in contradiction to His eternal production, but rather must be a perfect reflection of it. The eternal production of the Word was effected by a holy and purely spiritual power from a single principle, for which reason a similar production in time, from a single paternal principle, in a purely spiritual way, was in order.

The third reason concerns the dignity of Christ's humanity. In order that the human nature of the Savior be exempt from original sin, it was appropriate that it should not be formed by the ordinary process of human generation, but virginally. While, on the one hand, the bodily origin of the Savior had to be so arranged that, through it Christ actually comes in touch with the race, on the other hand He could not become dependent on its first head, nor share in the sin connected with that race. Above all, the flesh of Christ must be distinguished as a life-giving flesh, that is to say, as the seat and the instrument of God's life-giving Spirit. It was, therefore, to be formed by Him who alone could make it such and use it as the instrument of God's graces. The same idea is expressed in the writings of the French theologian, Louis Thomassin, who says: "The Bread of life, which bears in Itself the power of the Holy Spirit, has also to be prepared through the ardor of the same Holy Spirit."

The fourth and final reason has relation to the purpose for which Christ became man, namely, that men may be born unto children of God not "of the will of the flesh, nor of the will of man, but of God" (John 1:13), that is to say, by the very power of God, the exemplar of which should appear in the conception of Christ Himself. For which reason St. Augustine remarks: "It was fitting that the Head of humanity should be born of a virgin according to the flesh, in order that His birth might foreshadow the spiritual birth of His members, and be the prototype of the virginal motherhood of the Church."

St. Thomas posits still another question in relation to

the virginal conception, namely, whether it was proper at
all that Jesus should be born of a woman. Aside from the
fact that the human maternal production places the Savior
in direct contact with the human race, which He wished
to redeem by His Incarnation, the maternal production of
Christ offers one more advantage. These are the words of
St. Thomas: "Because the male sex is superior to the female sex, Christ assumed His human nature in the former.
Lest the female sex should be treated with neglect, He assumed His flesh from a woman." Thus the female sex
receives its own share in the elevation and glorification of
human nature, effected through the Incarnation. At the
same time an opportunity is offered to the female sex to
vindicate itself and avenge the unspeakable harm caused
by Eve. Here the words of St. Paul may be paraphrased:
As by the disobedience of one the many are constituted
sinners, so by the obedience of Mary the balance has been
restored, and many are constituted just. It is indeed significant, that the highest conceivable elevation of a created
person was achieved in Mary, surpassed only by the highest conceivable elevation of a created nature in the man,
Jesus Christ, when our Lord took flesh unto Himself and
was born of the Virgin Mary.

CHAPTER 5

MOTHER OF CHRIST

To appraise the relationship of Christ and His Mother
we must resort to a short explanation of our Lord's consecration as the Anointed of the Father.

From the prophecies of the Old Testament which refer to the coming of Christ we gather that the name of Christ, or the Anointed, has reference to the mystery of the Incarnation. Such is indicated by the words of Gabriel who explained to Daniel, the prophet, the mystical seventy weeks which were to precede the Incarnation. "Seventy weeks are shortened upon thy people, and upon thy holy city, that transgression may be finished, and sin may have an end, and iniquity may be abolished; and everlasting justice may be brought; and vision and prophecy may be fulfilled; *and the Saint of saints may be anointed*" (Dan. 9:24). There is no question of a material anointing, such as Aaron received when God chose him as the first high priest (Lev. 8:12). The anointing of Christ is purely spiritual. He was consecrated by the anointment of the hypostatic union, when the divinity was poured out upon His humanity to dwell in it incarnate. Christ's divinity so permeates and perfumes His humanity with its fragrance and life-giving power, that it extends its influence to others and fills them also with its power and fragrance. Christ received this anointment, as St. Paul states, at the time that He was vested with the dignity of the high priesthood, at the moment of His Incarnation, when God said to Him: "Thou art My Son, I this day have begotten Thee" (Heb. 5:5).

Christ's humanity is blessed in a singular manner. It received a threefold deification and sanctification. The initial and fundamental glory is bestowed upon His humanity by the hypostatic union, whereby Christ's human nature is deified as a nature belonging to God. Second, because of this union, the humanity of Christ is also transfigured and assimilated to God by grace and glory, wherein it participates with the fullness which is becoming to the

divine nature. And finally, as a corollary, there arises the
relation of the humanity to the divine Word, in virtue
of which it becomes the seat and the instrument of His
supernatural activity. All these mysteries may be combined
under the notion of anointing, by which the man in the
God-man becomes Christ, the Anointed. He is anointed,
not merely by divine mission for the discharge of an office,
not even merely by the outpouring of the Holy Spirit in
His deifying grace, but by personal union with God Himself. Accordingly, Christ and the God-man have an identical meaning. Both names express equally, in different
forms, the divine and incomprehensible mystery residing
in the person of Jesus. The name Jesus, which means Redeemer, signifies our Lord according to the function which
He has to exercise in behalf of men here on earth. But
the name Christ signifies His inner being and His direct,
personal relationship to God. Thus the Apostle speaks
of the "mystery of Christ" (Eph. 3:4), which was revealed
to him, and of "the unfathomable riches of Christ," which
Paul was to announce to the Gentiles, "to enlighten all
men as to what is the dispensation of the mystery which
has been hidden from eternity in God" (Eph. 3:9). Fundamentally the mystery of the Incarnation is nothing less
than the external prolongation of the mystery of the
Blessed Trinity, and a magnificent manifestation to the
outer world of the glory which was hidden from all eternity
in the Divinity itself.

To understand this, we must go back for a moment to
the mystery of the Blessed Trinity. The mystery of the
Blessed Trinity is explained fundamentally in the Nicene
Creed, which we read during Mass. "I believe in one Lord
Jesus Christ, the only-begotten Son of God . . . begotten,
not made; being of one substance with the Father . . .

and in the Holy Spirit, who proceeds from the Father and the Son." The term "begotten or generated" is employed to indicate that the production of the Second Person in God is wholly different from creation, by which God produces things outside Himself, and communicates to them an existence which is essentially different from His own existence. Generation is the highest form of production. By it the generating principle expresses itself in the most perfect manner and transplants its own essence and nature into the generated object. In the Holy Trinity the Son proceeds from the Father's innermost substance, which passes over to the Son and places Him in full possession of the nature which is proper to the Father. This generation is entirely intellectual and spiritual. The Father, as Father, turns inward to Himself and to His divine intelligence. He sees Himself and penetrates Himself with a gaze which wholly embraces His divine essence. The act whereby He knows Himself, and the Word whereby He emits Himself is the Son, His loving and substantial image, which He begets in eternity. Thus the Father remains within Himself in the unity of His essence, and goes out of Himself in the distinction of persons, and brings forth His interior Word by an intellectual generation. In this it differs from the production of the Third Person, who proceeds from the Father and the Son as the substantial expression of their mutual love, which is not called a generation, but rather a procession, or, as some theologians name it, a spiration.

Deep and mysterious as this inner manifestation of God within Himself remains, God willed that the interior communication of His nature and essence should be projected outside Himself in all its infinity. To this effect He willed that a bearer of created nature should be the bearer of His divine nature and essence as well. This could be done in no better way than that the Son, who had received the divine nature from Him from all eternity, should assume a human nature, thus enabling God to see His own natural image in a man and extend to a man the relationship of natural fatherhood, in which He stands to the Son in His bosom.

The procession of the Son from the Father in time is very similar to the eternal procession of the Word of God. Where the Eternal Word was generated unto the full essence and nature of the Father, the Incarnate Word came forth from His earthly mother really as the Son of God, in full possession of the very nature which is proper to the Father. Even the impregnating power, which the Angel described as the power of the Most High which overshadowed Mary, is God's own Holy Spirit which produced the Word of God. There are thus two generations in God, one in eternity and one in time. The second generation has its basis in the first, and the first virtually includes the second. This establishes interrelationship between the mystery of the Incarnation and the mystery of the Blessed Trinity to such an extent that the Incarnation has its explanation and its source in the Trinity, while the Trinity has its external prolongation and its highest meaning for the outer world in the Incarnation.

Thus the maternity of the Blessed Mother, as Cardinal Cajetan puts it, reaches even to the frontiers of Divinity. Christ, the Anointed of God, is given by the Eternal Father to the Virgin as her Son, and the unique holiness of His being, which is expressed in His name, is in a certain manner extended to His Virgin Mother and redounds to her glory, even as it shows forth the glory of God and His mercy in regard to humanity.

CHAPTER 6

MOTHER OF DIVINE GRACE

This title immediately follows that of "Mother of Christ." Thus the Litany combines the two and makes them, as it were, into one. If Mary is the Mother of Christ she is also Mother of divine grace, since she gave Christ to the world, or, as St. Thomas stated, "by bringing Him forth, she in a manner dispensed grace to all." This consideration, however fundamental, could not exhaust the beauty of the title, for it would leave Mary as a mere passive instrument in regard to grace. It would not emphasize Mary's active part in the distribution of grace. While the active distribution of grace is thus included in this title, we must limit ourselves in this chapter to the discussion of her personal graces, inasmuch as these graces prepared Mary for the sublime vocation which was hers by divine predestination.

These graces exceed all measure, as St. Thomas proclaims, when he says: "To be the worthy mother of God Mary needed to receive fullness of grace." This fullness expresses itself in a positive as well as in a negative manner.

The positive graces of Mary call for a parallel with the graces which each Christian receives because of his incorporation with Christ. The first and fundamental one, from which all others proceed, is habitual grace. It is received in the essence of the soul as a supernatural graft which elevates its spiritual growth. From this flow the theological and moral virtues, and the gifts of the Holy Spirit. These constitute a second nature and enable man to perform supernatural and meritorious acts, as it were, in a natural way. It makes men children of God, temples of the Most High, and entitles them to the actual and necessary graces which condition them to act in a manner becoming God's children. This life of grace is none other than eternal life begun on earth, which will outlive the passage of time and stay with us in eternity.

Mary's habitual grace, which matches ours in kind, exceeds ours in measure. This is quite understandable. Christ's own honor required that His Mother should receive a measure of grace which, as closely as possible, resembles His. Moreover, the love of God, whereby Mary in an unparalleled way becomes daughter, bride, and sanctuary of Divinity, requires that she be perfectly prepared for this association with God and receive grace in proportion. Because Christ was to take in her a bodily existence, her grace should be superabundant and be placed on the level of the hypostatic union. For, if habitual grace makes us adopted children of God, the divine maternity is by nature higher than adoptive sonship. Father Hugon remarks: "The former produces only a spiritual and mystic relationship, whereas the maternity of the Blessed Virgin establishes a relationship of nature, a relationship of consanguinity with Jesus Christ and one of affinity with the entire Trinity."

Thus, in preparing a sanctuary for His Son, the Father gave Mary a dignity in excess of all understanding and grace in excess of all measure. St. Thomas explains: "The humanity of Christ since it is united to God, the beatitude of the elect which is the possession of God, the Blessed Virgin Mary since she is the Mother of God—all these have a certain infinite dignity (and corresponding grace) from their relation to God Himself. Under this aspect there can be nothing more perfect than they because there can be nothing more perfect than God." St. Bonaventure supports this reasoning when he says: "God could make a greater world, but He cannot make a more perfect mother than the Mother of God."

Following the doctrine of St. Thomas, theologians enumerate a threefold form of this fullness of grace found in the Blessed Mother. One of disposition, by which she was made worthy to be the Mother of God. One of possession, by which she was made the actual repository of our Lord. One of consummation which corresponds to the fullness of glory which she now enjoys in heaven. The first form appears in her initial sanctification; the second confirmed her in grace; the third placed her in complete possession and direct fruition of all good.

This threefold distinction brings us to Mary's fullness of grace, considered in its negative aspect. The Church ascribes to Mary three privileges which have reference in some way to these three stages in Mary's life. The first has reference to her complete freedom from original sin. The second frees her from all the effects of original sin, and includes freedom from all inclination to sin and, in general, from all irregularity connected with the loss of original justice. The last privilege delivers Mary from the reign of death inasmuch as death is a consequence of original sin and the cause of the decomposition of the body.

The ancient axiom, "As the Lamb, so is the Mother of the Lamb," is completely realized in the negative side of Mary's privileges. Whatever, by the power of the divine Word, is to be unconditionally excluded from Christ's human nature, is also incompatible with the person of Mary as the Mother of Christ. If Christ was completely preserved from sin and from whatever is so connected with sin that it defaces in man the image of God, so was Mary, the Mother of Christ. If in Christ there was no inclination to sin, no general deformity as to mind and will—such as was in Adam because of the fall—so in Mary there was infused knowledge, freedom from all error, control of the passions, and total absence of the disturbing influences of sensuality. If, finally, Christ conquered death and the reign of death and, by His glorious resurrection, extended eternal incorruption to His sacred humanity, so Mary was exempt from the bonds of death to the extent that her body remained free from corruption. The one exception—that Christ freely accepted physical suffering and death for Himself, in punishment for the sin of humanity and as a means of redemption—made it all the more necessary that His Mother, His associate and His helper in the work of redemption, should also be subject to both.

All these graces came to Mary because of the merits of her Son, either anticipated or applied after they were actually gained. Without the merits of Christ's redemption Mary would have been subject to all these penalties of sin like every other human being. But, through the merits of our Lord, her's, like Christ's, was a complete victory over sin and the devil, according to the words of the Protevangelium: "I will put enmities between thee and the woman, and thy seed and her seed" (Gen. 3:15). Thus was realized the twin blessedness of Mother and Son, as proclaimed by Elizabeth in the words: "Blessed art thou among women and blessed is the fruit of thy womb" (Luke 1:42).

As a final observation, we may compare Mary's fullness of grace with the absolute fullness of grace which Christ possessed in His human nature; and with the relative fullness of grace which is the portion of the saints, as essential to their particular degree of perfection.

In Christ the fullness of grace was absolute, as becomes the Savior of mankind. It is the inexhaustible source of all the graces which all men have received since the fall of Adam, or will receive till the end of time. There can be no greater grace than this.

There is the relative fullness of grace of the elect, or the fullness of sufficiency, which enables them to perform those meritorious acts which will determine their future degree of glory with its corresponding degree of eternal happiness.

Finally, there is Mary's fullness of grace, which is one of superabundance, which increased up to the time of her death, and which has ever since been poured on the souls of men. Compared with the wealth of other saints, Mary's fullness is beyond measure and degree, for it is overflowing, as some theologians say, "a plenitude of redundance." This privilege can and does enable Mary to cooperate effectively, and by virtue of her own activity, in the distribution of grace to others.

CHAPTER 7

MOTHER MOST PURE

Purity, as a supernatural virtue, is of divine origin. It is a hidden flower in God's garden of virtues, which Divinity tended for an eternity past, for it reflects its own Being more than any other. But today, purity is planted in out-of-the-way places, and wherever it blooms there is a bit of heaven, a hidden corner of paradise.

Purity is called the angelic virtue, for it lifts a person above the desires of the flesh and makes human nature resemble that of the angels. In fact, those who live a life of purity are superior to the angels, because humans have the flesh to combat, which the angels have not.

Those who live a pure life are extremely pleasing to God. It is well known that our Lord loved little children because of their simplicity and purity of heart, and He showed a particular predilection for those who in this virtue resembled little children. He chose a pure virgin for His mother; a man of angelic purity for His foster-father. John the Baptist, who was purified in his mother's womb, was His precursor. The Apostle John, because of his purity, was particularly intimate with Jesus, as his title of Beloved Disciple indicates. He was privileged at the Last Supper to rest upon Jesus' breast, and, beneath the Cross, our Lord entrusted to him the care of His Virgin Mother. "He that loves cleanness of heart shall have the king for his friend," says the Book of Proverbs (22:11). Purity of heart is health to the soul and light to the understanding. It is the aid to the attainment of wisdom and imparts knowledge, which can well explain how John was able to penetrate so deeply into the mysteries of faith and of the Divinity itself, and that the gates of heaven were opened to him in his vision of Patmos.

In Mary this attractive virtue attained to new heights and still greater splendor. In her the virtue of purity assumed the special beauty of virginal chastity, which was made absolute by the perfection of the vow.

The formal element of virginity, as mentioned before, is the purpose of perpetually preserving perfect chastity by abstaining from sexual pleasure, whether from lust or from the lawful use of marriage. Ordinarily this purpose is inspired by a virtue superior to that of chastity: the motive being either religious, or apostolic, or simply inspired by the virtue of divine love. The superior virtue will ennoble this purpose and communicate to it its own beauty. The resolution is generally offered to God in the form of a vow.

Although not spoken of in the Old Testament the counsel of virginity is expressly given in the New Testament. Christ reminded His disciples that besides those who are unfit for marriage by nature, or by reason of a mutilation inflicted by men, we find others who have made the same sacrifice for the kingdom of heaven. Our Lord recommended them to imitate the latter, saying: "Let him accept it who can" (Matt. 19:12). Tradition has always understood this text in the sense of an invitation to perpetual continence. St. Paul formally declares that marriage is honorable, but that it would be better to follow his counsel and remain single (I Cor. 7:25–40). The Church, following this teaching of the Apostle, considers the state of virginity preferable in itself to the state of marriage. For the state of virginity marks a signal victory over the lower appetites, an emancipation of worldly cares, and furnishes an opportunity to devote oneself explicitly to the things of God. The Council of Trent pronounces an anathema against the opposite doctrine.

Aside from the fact that perfect integrity of the body, enhanced by a purpose of perpetual chastity, produces a special likeness to Christ and was most fitting for the Mother of Christ, we have special proof, established by Sacred Scripture, that Mary did take a vow of perpetual virginity. The answer to the Angel, "How shall this happen, since I do not know man" (Luke 1:34), does not permit of any explanation other than this, that Mary at that moment had already bound herself by vow to keep her virginity intact. Neither do Our Lady's betrothal and subsequent marriage to Joseph in any way contradict this vow, as some authors would have it. Her quality of virgin consecrated to God, could with equal reason question the reality of her marriage. Some theologians have suggested that her vow was at first conditional, since she was not certain that the keeping of her virginity under all circumstances would be pleasing to God. While this supposition does not destroy the moral integrity of her vow, we may well suppose that even this surmise is unwarranted. Mary trusted divine guidance implicitly, and thus was certain that her vow could be kept even in the married state. As such her vow fulfilled all requirements necessary to the formal perfection of the vow. It expressed her undivided loyalty to God, the chief aim of virginity, and an unrestricted and complete surrender, which constitutes the soul of the vow. When we suppose that God prepared Mary for her sublime vocation by the infusion of a virginal inclination, we may well agree that her vow contained from the beginning the formal element which includes a firm purpose to retain it forever. In this manner it joined to the permanent and perfect virginity of the body of Mary, a truth defined by the Church, an attitude of mind which some theologians call virginity of spirit.

As an additional distinction of Mary's vow it is usually thought to have been the first one ever taken. This opinion cannot be proved in a positive way. Yet it is very probable, considering that Jewish maidens aspired after marriage as the accomplishment of a natural duty. In consideration of the divine decree that the Messiah should arise out of

Israel, the urge to propagate the people of God took a relative precedence over the observance of virginity. Not that the thought of freely chosen perpetual virginity was strange to the Israelites even before the time of Christ. Most of the Essenes—a religious sect which originated around 150 B.C.—rejected marriage as a matter of convenience. But we cannot prove, or even suppose on the strength of the aforesaid consideration, that other maidens before Mary had both made the resolution and taken the formal vow of virginity.

The virginal vow, which includes a subjective engagement on the part of Mary to become God's spiritual bride, was formally accepted, and objectively consecrated when God took Mary and united her to Himself as His bride. In this, her vow differs from vows taken by others. Contemplating as it does a supernatural marriage with God, the taking of the vow remains for others totally a spiritual engagement. In Mary, originating as such, it found its final term in her becoming the actual bride of God. There is still another difference. In others the acceptance of the vow by the Church as Christ's representative, constitutes its formal sanction. In Mary, the conception of Christ is rightly regarded as the consecration of herself and her virginity, and constitutes the formal solemnization of her vow.

In final confirmation of Mary's vow of virginity we have the special feast in the Church calendar, which celebrates her Presentation in the Temple (Nov. 21). This feast emphasizes a vow of Mary, made in the Temple at an early age. Although the feast is mentioned in the Eastern Church for the first time in a document of 1166, and found introduction in the Western Church in 1371—the special office being of an even later date—we cannot deny a certain degree of authority to this observance, which must have found its origin in a very ancient tradition. At any rate, the old adage, "Lex orandi est lex credendi," which may be freely translated, "Whatever the Church sanctions by her liturgy finds its foundation in faith," demands at least that we treat with reverence the suggestions contained in her liturgical prayers.

CHAPTER 8

MOTHER MOST CHASTE

While the preceding title emphasizes Mary's virginal purity, the present one gives due glory to her connubial chastity. There is a close relationship between the two, inasmuch as the latter finds its origin in Mary's vow of virginity and was sanctified by it.

In discussing the general topic of her virginal maternity, St. Thomas posits two questions relative to Our Lady's married state. The first one inquires if it is proper that Christ should be born of a married virgin; the second discusses the reality of the marriage between Mary and Joseph.

The reasons given for the convenience of this marriage of the Blessed Mother are listed by St. Thomas under three headings. He discusses her marriage as pertinent to our Lord's dignity, as becoming to Mary herself, and as appropriate in our regard.

That the marriage of Mary was in keeping with the dignity of the Child is beyond question. Apart from the fact that Christ should not be deprived of a proper genealogy,

derived from a legal father, His human birth out of wed-
lock would have been disgraceful in the eyes of both Jews
and Gentiles. The necessity of a legal father is further
emphasized by the fact that Christ as well as the mother
needed someone who could care for them in the proper
way. St. Ignatius adds as a fourth reason, that Christ's mysterious birth should be kept hidden from the devil, at
least during His early years. In explanation of this St.
Thomas brings in the authority of St. Augustine, who
claims supernatural intervention to prevent the devil from
knowing the mystery of the Incarnation, in order to safe-
guard the Child Jesus against unnecessary embarrassment
or persecution at the age when, by divine decree, He would
be helpless and unable to manifest His power over the
devil.

It was also fitting that Mary should have entered the
married state at the time that she carried and brought forth
her Son. By being married legally she assured herself of
the natural protection and loving care of St. Joseph, at a
moment when her honor could be challenged and her good
name endangered. Besides, there was a death penalty, prescribed by law, not only for those unfaithful in marriage,
but also for those who, before marriage, were found guilty
of unlawful sexual relations (Deut. 22:21).

That Mary's marriage was appropriate also in our regard is evident from the fact that it gives additional proof
of her virginal conception, as attested by her own words:
"How shall this happen, since I do not know man" (Luke
1:34), as well as by Joseph's reaction when he found the
mother with child and was reassured by the Angel. Although a bit lengthy, we give the complete text: "When
Mary His mother had been betrothed to Joseph, she was
found, before they came together, to be with child by the

Holy Spirit. But Joseph her husband, being a just man, and not wishing to expose her to reproach, was minded to put her away privately. But while he thought on these things, behold, an angel of the Lord appeared to him in a dream, saying: "Do not be afraid, Joseph, son of David, to take to thee Mary thy wife, for that which is begotten in her is of the Holy Spirit. And she shall bring forth a son, and thou shalt call His name Jesus; for He shall save His people from their sins" (Matt. 1:18–21). St. Thomas finds a final proof of the appropriateness of Mary's connubial standing in its symbolic meaning, since her virginal marriage affected the dignity of the Universal Church, which, being in the virginal state, is married to Christ.

The second question, which discusses the real marriage of Mary and Joseph, is treated at length by St. Thomas. At the outset, we should establish the fact that Mary's vow of virginity does not exclude the possibility of a real marriage. On the contrary, we must claim that, under the circumstances a real marriage between Mary and Joseph was necessary, because of the several reasons mentioned above. There are, indeed, two kinds of marriages. One, which we may call a non-virginal marriage, which has as primary purpose the procreation of mankind; and the virginal marriage, which has as its primary purpose the mutual support of the contracting parties. That the latter deserves the name of a real marriage as well as the first, is established by St. Thomas who cites the fact that a marriage in which both contracting parties, by mutual consent decide to refrain from using their marriage rights, still remains a marriage, and is truly considered as such.

It might be objected that from a virginal marriage the basic right of using the fundamental privileges of a natural marriage cannot be excluded. In reality, the marriage of Mary and Joseph did not eliminate the fundamental purpose of procreation. It only transferred this primary end of marriage to another and entirely supernatural sphere. In every marriage a twofold perfection is to be considered: one which concerns the form of the marriage contract, and the other which considers the end or purpose of marriage. The perfection of the form consists in the mutual agreement of the contracting parties to become so bound to one another that henceforth they form one indissoluble whole, as an instrument belonging to God and taken possession of by God for the joint achievement of a service. This joint service, which is connected with the very purpose of marriage, usually has regard to the combined act of procreation, and the subsequent obligation of caring for the offspring. In a natural marriage the last mentioned obligation is dependent on the first. Nothing, however, prevented God from using the marriage of Mary and Joseph as a means to attain the secondary end, independent of the first. In this respect the bond which brought Mary and Joseph together in marriage was not entirely of the same nature as the bond of ordinary marriages. But the perfection of this bond was by far greater and holier, inasmuch as it was effected by divine decree in order to give a joint service to God, which by far excelled the service given to God in ordinary marriage, namely the care of God's only-begotten Son.

That both Mary and Joseph gave free consent to this joint service, which made their marriage eminently fruitful, is evident from the words of Holy Scripture. Mary gave full consent to her supernatural conception when she spoke the deciding words: "Behold the handmaid of the Lord; be it done to me according to thy word" (Luke 1:38).

Joseph accorded his when he did as the Angel commanded and took Mary unto himself, after the true nature of her conception was explained to him. Even though the fruit was not produced in the regular, natural way, it still belonged to both, by virtue of the spiritual unity of husband and wife. This also throws greater light on the true character of their marriage. Although it was a union which excluded the radical marriage rights from the beginning in an actual and formal way, it was more than a bond of friendship, or protection, or even of simple betrothal. Contracted by God's special authorization, it had all the essential characteristics of a real marriage. This also affords a deeper understanding of the paternity of St. Joseph, which was a true paternity, resting as it did upon God's own decree and upon the perfection of his marriage with the bodily mother of the Child.

In accordance with the mind of the Church, we must finally concede to Mary that virginity of heart which, along with her absolute perfect virginity, enhanced the beauty of her marriage contract. This glorifies the moral perfection and holiness of her will, which was at all time in total agreement with God, and forms the foundation of the special feast which the Church celebrates on August 22, to honor the Immaculate Heart of Mary.

CHAPTER 9

MOTHER INVIOLATE

Mary's bodily integrity which remained untouched when she conceived Jesus Christ has been well established.

The absolute perfection of the virginity of the Mother of Christ now demands that we prove that she remained inviolate while bringing forth her divine Son.

Before we attempt an adequate explanation of the mystery, we should state the absolute, dogmatic stand of the Church concerning this question. According to traditional teaching the Church holds that, through the supernatural influence of the Holy Spirit, Mary gave birth to her Son in such a manner that the bodily integrity of the mother was in no wise violated, and that she retained her virginity in the act of childbirth, as much as she retained it when she conceived.

The mystery was prefigured in olden times by the East Gate of the new Temple, seen by the prophet in vision, which remained closed permanently. And the Lord said to him: "This gate shall be shut, it shall not be opened, and no man shall pass through it: because the Lord the God of Israel has entered in by it" (Ezech. 44:2). The Fathers of the early Church found in these words of Ezechiel a reference to Mary, the Gate of salvation, through which Christ came into the world.

The doctrine is formally defined in the third canon of the Lateran Council, which states: "If anyone does not profess that Mary is truly and appropriately the holy mother of God, immaculate and ever a virgin, since the Word of God is conceived of the Holy Spirit without seed and *is brought forth incorruptibly,* let him be anathema."

The prophecy of Isaias, "Behold a virgin shall conceive, and bear a son" (Is. 7:14), is likewise very conclusive. Understood in a composite sense, the virginity of Mary is attested to in both her conception and in her childbirth, and hailed by the prophet in its combined aspect, as a great sign and miracle. The original text, which reads, "Behold a virgin pregnant and giving birth," is even more explicit.

To this may be added the words of St. Leo, which were accepted by the Council of Chalcedon as a part of the official declaration: "Christ is conceived of the Holy Spirit within the womb of the virgin mother who brought Him forth without embarrassment of her virginity." And the words of St. Augustine: "If Mary's integrity were violated by Christ's birth, then surely He was not born of a virgin. It would be wrong for the whole Church to profess, as it does now, that Christ is born of the Virgin Mary. The Church itself, imitating the Mother of God, daily begets members, yet remains a virgin."

If Mary could conceive without embarrassment to her virginity, she could likewise bring forth without injury of her bodily integrity, for the latter is but a natural supplement of her virginal conception. It appears much like the miracle performed by Christ at the time of His resurrection, when He came forth from the grave which remained closed and securely sealed. It also shows points of conformity with Christ's passage through locked doors on Easter Sunday. These two miracles, however, while they illustrate do not fully explain the present mystery, since Christ's body coming forth from His mother, lacked the subtlety of His glorified body after the resurrection. Following the example of St. Thomas we confine ourselves to ascribing the miracle directly to a special intervention of the power of God, which, substantially dwelling in the body of Christ, enabled Him to penetrate the limits of nature without violating them. As such it demonstrates both the reality of Christ's body and His divine power, as well as His ability to combine both in one. The Angelic Doctor remarks: "In order to show that His body was real, He was born of a woman; but in order to show His divinity, He was born of a virgin."

In view of the preceding consideration, we are obliged to read St. Luke's narrative of the Presentation of the Child Jesus in the Temple with a great deal of caution and mental reserve. When the Evangelist mentions that the days of Mary's purification were fulfilled, we cannot interpret these words too literally. Likewise, when he represents the offering of Jesus as the fulfillment of the precept of Moses regarding "every male opening the womb," we cannot infer that Mary's Child had actually opened the womb of His Mother in the conventional way. In both instances St. Luke cites the wording of a Jewish law to which neither our Lord nor Mary was obliged under the circumstances, but which Mary decided to observe for a double reason. First, in order to hide the supernatural character of the birth of her Child. Second, in order to show due respect to the Law. In this, Mary was but following the future example of her Son, who Himself would testify in later years: "Do not think that I have come to destroy the Law and the Prophets. I have not come to destroy, but to fulfill" (Matt. 5:17).

For the purpose of illustrating that a virginal birth is the only birth proper to the Son of God, St. Thomas explains it as entirely consonant with the eternal birth of the divine Word in the bosom of the Father. For, the divine Word, which was conceived without corruption of His substance, was generated by the Father without any harm inflicted on His integrity. The human mind generates the word in which it expresses its idea much in the same manner. In this respect Theodore of Ancyra remarked in a sermon, given at the Council of Ephesus: "The divine Word, while being born in the flesh, safeguarded His Mother's virginity, thereby showing His true nature of divine Word."

A virginal birth was also appropriate because of the effect it produced in regard to us. For Christ came on earth to remove the damage done to our human nature. In this process it would have veen very unlikely that He would have brought detriment to His mother's virginity, which was her most prized possession. Says St. Augustine: "It would not have been proper that the birth of our Lord, who came to heal corruption, would have violated integrity." To this St. Thomas adds as a final consideration, that He, who commands us to honor our parents, could least of all have suffered an impairment of the glory of Mary by allowing the ravages of a natural motherhood.

The absolute perfection of the bodily virginity of the Mother of Jesus is usually thus defined: Mary was a virgin in the birth of her Son, before the birth, and after the birth. The order shows that Mary's integrity was miraculously preserved in the birth of Jesus as a due reflection of her virginal conception. It also guarantees the perpetual continuation of her integrity, as a part of her perfect virginity, to the exclusion of any other human conception. This constitutes the subject matter of our next chapter.

CHAPTER 10

MOTHER UNDEFILED

With the Church we accept the absolute perfection of Mary's virtue, and profess, along with the virginal conception and birth of our Lord, a continuation of Mary's virginity throughout her life. Here also we have the dogmatic definition of the Church, given at the Council of Lateran. "If anyone does not profess . . . that Mary's virginity remained intact after the birth of our Lord, let him be anathema."

Once again the text of Ezechiel which mentions the "closed gate" is referred to as an intrinsic reason, demonstrating the propriety of Mary's perpetual virginity. By way of example we quote an excerpt of a letter written by St. Ambrose to Pope Siricius, in the name of the Council of Milan. It reads as follows: "Who is that gate of the sanctuary, that outward gate which looks to the east, which remains shut, and through which no man shall pass, except the God of Israel Himself? Is not Mary that gate, through which the Redeemer entered into the world?" St. Augustine goes on to say: "What else does the closed gate suggest, but that Mary remained forever intact? No man shall pass through it. Does it not mean that Joseph will not know her? The Lord alone enters and departs by it. Does it not signify that the Holy Spirit will impregnate her, and the Lord of Angels will be born of her? The gate will be closed forever. Does it not mean that Mary is a virgin before childbirth, in childbirth, and remains a virgin thereafter?"

The constant and perpetual virginity of Mary is indicated in Sacred Scripture by several details. First and foremost is her vow of virginity, the existence of which was clearly attested to, when Mary inquired of the Angel: "How shall this happen, since I do not know man?" (Luke 1:34) That this vow was absolute and unconditional, and assumed the dignity of a solemn vow when it was ratified by God Himself in the mystery of the Incarnation, has been established previously. Here we add that Mary is continuously mentioned in the Gospel as the Mother of Jesus;

and that, for want of other sons, our dying Lord bequeathed to her the services of St. John, the Beloved Disciple, who was himself a virgin.

When the Church addresses Our Lady not merely as Virgin, but as Virgin of virgins, she simply confirms the established tradition that Mary, as the Mother of Christ and the outstanding example of virginity, remained forever inviolate and undefiled. Since the virginal disposition of Mary after conception is a necessary result of this conception, and the absence of it would have been a grievous sin, the Fathers treated the denial of this truth with the greatest indignation.

The few exegetical difficulties raised by heretics are hardly relevant, and have been sufficiently solved by St. Jerome. They chiefly concern three expressions of Sacred Scripture which could be damaging to our doctrine, if the opposing theory were not dogmatically defined and generally accepted. Besides, there is a plausible explanation for each one of them.

The first one is about the words of St. Matthew's Gospel, "And he did not know her till she had brought forth her firstborn Son" (Matt. 1:25). The words ought to be read in connection with the preceding passage where Joseph is told by the Angel to take unto him Mary his wife, as she had conceived from the Holy Spirit. St. Chrysostom gives a rather pleasing explanation of the passage. "Before she brought forth her Son," he says, "Joseph did not know Mary in her true value and dignity. After the Incarnation he did know her, and she became to him by far more priceless and far more esteemed than the entire world, because she had held within her womb Him, whom the entire world cannot contain." Even if we have to assign to the expression the usual Biblical meaning, the conjunc-

tion "until" in Holy Scripture does not of necessity indicate the cessation of a previously existing state of affairs.
Thus, when we read in the Book of Psalms: "Our eyes are
unto the Lord our God, until He has mercy on us" (Ps.
122:2), we do not wish to infer that after God has shown
mercy we shall turn our eyes away from Him. The words
of the Evangelist must be understood in a similar manner.
The passage simply indicates that Joseph did not know
Mary in a marital way before she brought forth her Child,
without any implication as to the future.

The very term "first-born son" has caused confusion in
the minds of some. It is found in the above mentioned
context, and appears repeatedly in the Gospel. In itself the
expression excludes only former sons, and is not at all in-
dicative of later children. On this point the Bible is clear.
When the Mosaic Law says: "Sanctify unto Me every first-
born" (Exo. 13:2), the corresponding passage (Num. 18:16)
demands that this be done after one month, which excludes all possible reference to future offspring.

The last difficulty, which refers to the fact that several
persons are mentioned in the Gospel as the "brothers of
Jesus," cannot be misunderstood even by one who is only
slightly familiar with the Hebrew language. The expression is often used in a wide sense to include all near and
even distant relatives. Thus St. James, who particularly
is mentioned as the brother of the Lord (Gal. 1:19) was
the son of Alpheus, and a cousin of Jesus.

Having looked at these exegetical difficulties, and refused them any importance, we return to St. Thomas, who
treats the absurdity of the opposing view in a conclusively
thorough manner. His argument is chiefly against Hel-
vidius and the Antidicomarianites, who claimed that the
Mother of God had other children by Joseph after she

had borne Jesus. This opinion has been revived in modern times, and is adopted by many Protestant exegetes. St. Thomas wished to prove that their error was opposed to the dignity of Christ. For, since He is the only Son in eternity of the Father, so He ought to be in time the only Son of the virgin. The contrary belief is a slight also to the honor of the Holy Spirit, Mary's divine Bridegroom, who sanctified her womb once and for all, and kept her as His exclusive temple. It would have cast a cloud on the nobility of character and the unsurpassed holiness of the Mother of God, if she had shown dissatisfaction with being the mother of the Only-begotten of the Father, and had given up her virginity, which had been preserved in her in such a miraculous manner, in favor of other children. Joseph, lastly, would have been guilty of the greatest temerity had he violated the virginity of her whom he knew by the word of the Angel, to have conceived of the Holy Spirit. Thus, St. Thomas concludes, it must be said without qualification that the Mother of God conceived as a virgin, brought forth as a virgin, and remained a virgin ever after.

CHAPTER II

MOTHER MOST AMIABLE

Now that we have considered Mary's prerogatives as mother and virgin, we return to some of her privileges which are directly derived from her exalted position, according to the eternal plans of God. Mary is most amiable and exceedingly pleasing to both God and men. As such this beautiful title is full of charm, and describes not only God's love for Mary, but, as a necessary corollary, it gives expression to our love for her as well.

The sequence and substance of God's plan of redemption are summarized by Pope Pius IX in his Bull *Ineffabilis*. These are his words: "From the beginning and before all ages God selected and prepared for His only Son the Mother from whom, having taken flesh, He would be born in the blessed fullness of time. He loved her by herself more than all creatures, and with such a love as to find His delight in her in a singular way. Drawing from the treasures of His divinity, He endowed her, more than all the angels and saints, with such an abundance of heavenly gifts that she was always completely free from sin, and that, all beautiful and perfect, she appeared in such a plenitude of innocence and holiness that, except God's, no greater than hers can be conceived, and that no mind but the mind of God can measure it." Thus, in the sequence or order of God's plan, He first chose Mary to be the Mother of His Son. In consequence of that selection, He equipped her with a fullness of grace which would prepare her to be a worthy mother. Indeed Mary needed this fullness of grace so that, from the first instant, she could conceive her Son in holiness and give her consent with the utmost generosity on the day of the Annunciation, in spite of the sufferings which she knew had been foretold of the Messiah. She needed it, that she might conceive and bring forth her Child with her virginity remaining intact; that she might surround Him with the most motherly and most holy devotion during His hidden life; that she might be enabled to make her supreme sacrifice, and unite herself to Him in closest conformity of will when He hung on

the Cross and she witnessed His last, heart-rending struggle.

That Mary's fullness of grace exceeded all measure is
well confirmed by the words of Pius IX. It exceeded the
treasure of grace of all angels and saints together, and was
indeed so great that "no greater grace than hers can be
conceived and that no mind except the mind of God can
measure it." The divine maternity demands an exceedingly high degree of intimate friendship with God, as
Father Bossuet notes in his sermon on the conception of
the Blessed Mother: "God so loved the world, as to give
His only begotten Son. But the ineffable love which He
had for you, O Mary, exceeded His love for the world.
He ordained that He should belong to you in the same
quality in which He belonged to Himself. In order to
establish an eternal union with you, He made you the
Mother of His only Son and Himself the Father of yours.
O abyss of charity! What mind does not find itself lost
when it considers the incomprehensible regard He had for
you. You come nearer to Him than any other through this
Son common to you both. Through this inviolable bond
of sacred alliance, through this pledge of mutual love by
which the Father gave the Son to you in His impassible
divinity, you returned Him to the Father in His mortal
flesh."

Since the love of God is a sanctifying love, there was
never any moment in the life of Mary in which she did
not grow in love. Every successive act of love made her
more lovable and more attractive in the eyes of God. This
progress in love was the more continuous as it encountered
no obstacle. Physical science tells us that the velocity of a
falling body increases gradually and constantly the nearer
it approaches its term. This is an image of the growth of

charity in a soul which allows nothing to hold it back. It
moves faster toward God according as the increasing near-
ness to Him increases His attraction. Mary's grace and holiness exceeded all measure from the beginning, and were
ever increased by her constant association with the One
who is the very source of grace, and who loved her as only
a son can love his mother.

If God's special love for Mary is founded upon her
singular privilege of being the Mother of God, our love
for her finds its foundation in the very same prerogative.
Evidently, Mary is not our mother in the ordinary sense
of the term, since she did not give us natural life. But she
did give us supernatural life in union with her divine Son.
Like God's fatherhood in regard to the just, Mary's maternity is adoptive. But it really and effectively participates in the fecundity and the fruitfulness of the Godhead
and communicates grace, which is the germ of eternal life.
This maternity is universal and includes the whole of humanity, just as our Lord's redemption is universal; but
Mary's first love goes out to the faithful, to all those who
believe in her Son and receive from Him the life of grace.
This mark of distinction Abbot Marmion calls "Mary's
special grace of maternity toward Christ's mystical body."
For, when Mary conceived Jesus she conceived also His
members: all those who cannot be separated from Him,
that is to say, all the regenerate and all those who are called
to incorporation with Him. In other words, when Mary
became mother of Jesus according to the flesh, she also became mother of men according to the spirit. The natural
consequence of the Incarnation is to confer on men the
right and the power to become children of God. Sacred
Scripture has pointed this out in no uncertain terms. Says
St. Paul: "When the fullness of time came, God sent His

Son, born of a woman . . . that we might receive the adoption of sons" (Gal. 4:4–5). It is through the Word who joined human nature to Himself by means of the flesh, that we are joined to the Father: directly by the Son, indirectly by the Mother, who gave us the Son. Thus, in strictest sense our Lord is the chief meritorious cause of all the graces which we receive as adopted children. But Mary, who associated herself so closely with Him, in the sense that she enabled Him to accomplish this mission, has merited with Him, not in the same degree, but secondarily and in the manner which theologians call "de congruo," that is to say, under Christ and because of Him. This expression has been ratified by Blessed Pope Pius X, who declares that Mary has merited for us by right of congruity all the graces which Jesus has merited "de condigno," or by right of justice.

These graces she merited first of all at the moment of the Incarnation. It was by her free consent to become the Mother of the Savior, that she became the Mother of divine grace and of our spiritual regeneration. She would still have been our spiritual mother, as the result of this free acceptance of God's will and divine plan had she died before her Son. But this was not the case. Instead she lived on, in accord with God's design, that she might associate herself still more closely and more intimately with the work of the Redemption. She brought up Jesus, she nourished Him, and prepared Him to be the Victim of Calvary. Hers was a hidden life of love and suffering, such as was never equaled by any human being. The culmination of her life of sacrifice came at Calvary when she acquiesced in the death of her Son, suffering in her soul what Jesus suffered in His body, uniting herself with her Son as a victim for our sins. It has been truly said that, as Mary stood beneath the Cross Christ poured forth all His redeeming blood into the heart of the mother from whom He had received it, so that through her, as through a channel, it could flow over all mankind. Indeed, Mary cooperated in the redemption as only a mother can cooperate. She did it with a heartfelt gratitude for the privilege of being allowed to participate in the sacrifice of her Son, which was to save the world.

It was also on Calvary that our Lord ratified His previous selection and proclaimed Mary as our Mother in a most solemn manner. When He gave her to St. John with the words: "Behold thy mother" (John 19:27), He gave her also to us in the same capacity. Tradition has consistently understood these words in this sense. They do not refer to a grace peculiar to St. John, but go beyond him to all who are to be regenerated by the sacrifice of the Cross. The words of the dying Savior thus assumed the importance of a last will and testament, and produced in effect what they signified. In Mary's soul they meant an increase of charity and maternal love for her children. In us, as in St. John, they brought about a more profound filial affection for the one who gave us Jesus, and with Him the beauty and all the graces of the interior life.

CHAPTER 12

MOTHER MOST ADMIRABLE

Our Lord is the chief meritorious cause of all the graces which we receive as adopted children, He is also the chief exemplary cause of our sanctification. In Him we are called to imitate the Father after His own example: "For those whom God has foreknown He has also predestined to become conformed to the image of His Son, that He should be the firstborn among many brethren" (Rom. 8:29). In her transcendental position as Mother of the Savior Mary appears next to, and immediately after Christ. She, too, displays a striking image and likeness of God, to such a degree that the Church does not hesitate to place her before the faithful as the secondary and most beautiful exemplar of all virtues.

In this sense, St. Grignon de Montfort quotes St. Augustine, who calls Mary the living mold of God. In her the God-man was formed, and in her alone can man become like unto God. Whoever is in this mold and allows himself to be formed there, takes on the appearance of our Lord in a manner adapted to his human weakness, without excess of pain or labor. This is a safe way, without danger of illusion. For Satan never had and never will have power over Mary, nor will his power be excessive in regard to those who reproduce in themselves her characteristics, and who try to reach the image of the Son through the example of the Mother. This is the reason why theologians commonly teach that a true devotion to Mary, which consists in loving her to the extent of her example, is one of the signs of predestination. It cannot be forgotten that devotion means devotedness, and devotedness means the gift of self. Thus, we shall be devoted to Mary if we give ourselves entirely to her and through her to God. In so doing we imitate God who gives Himself and His Son to us through Mary. Blessed Hugh of Saint-Cher goes so far as to say that Mary is, as it were, the book of life or the mirror of that eternal book, since God has written in her the names of all the elect, just as He has willed to form in her and by her the Only-begotten of the Father, who is the first of the elect.

To name only a few of Mary's principal virtues as they are mentioned in the Gospel, hers was a deep faith. She believed the marvels which the Angel announced to her at her humble abode of Nazareth without hesitation, nor for one moment did she doubt the words of Gabriel, as Zachary had done; although she prudently inquired how it should be accomplished, since she had resolved to remain a virgin and did not know man. She was commended for this faith by her cousin, St. Elizabeth, who soon after would say: "Blessed is she who has believed, because the things promised to her by the Lord shall be accomplished" (Luke 1:45). In Bethlehem she beheld her Son born in a stable and believed that He is the Creator of the universe; she saw all the weakness of His infant body yet believed in His omnipotence; she took flight into Egypt to evade the treachery of King Herod and believed that "the government is upon His shoulder, that His empire shall be multiplied, and that He shall sit upon the throne of David, and upon his kingdom" (Is. 9:6–7). "Faith," the Apostle writes, "is the substance of things hoped for, the evidence of things that are not seen" (Heb. 11:1). Mary's entire life on earth was spent in that dark brightness of faith: the darkness of the unintelligible mystery of the redemption, and the brightness of its inner meaning, its appropriateness, its consequences. Even at the foot of the Cross she stood erect, firm in her faith that her Son is the Lamb of God who even then was taking away the sins of the world. Indeed, Mary's act of faith on Calvary was the strongest of all, for the hour was exceedingly dark and the powers of evil unmistakably evident, yet she believed that this apparent defeat of her

Son meant actual victory over Satan and sin, and would mean victory over death on the third day.

Turning back to Mary's visit of Elizabeth we find a striking example of humility. Rather than biding her time after the Annunciation in contemplation of the beautiful thing which was about to take place, she hastened into the hill country, to a town of Juda, in order to congratulate her cousin Elizabeth, and to render whatever assistance she could to this woman, who for many years had been barren and now expected a son in her old age. Hardly being outdone by Mary's kindness, Elizabeth recognized the outstanding dignity which was Mary's as the mother of the Messiah, and praised her accordingly. It was then that Our Lady replied with the immortal hymn of the *Magnificat,* the words of which are enshrined in the heart of every Christian: "My soul magnifies the Lord, and my spirit rejoices in God my Savior; because He has regarded the lowliness of His handmaid. . . . He has scattered the proud in the conceit of their heart. He has put down the mighty from their thrones, and has exalted the lowly" (Luke 1:46–52).

In the event that we desire to contemplate Mary's trust and confidence in her Son, we may point at the scene of Christ's first miracle at Cana of Galilee. It occurred among a group of kindly people who had invited some friends and relatives to a wedding feast. They were at the point of being embarrassed because of lack of wine, when Mary turned to her Son with a remark which could hardly be called a suggestion, far less a request. When our Lord objected to her kind interference because His hour had not yet come, Mary was not to be discouraged and said to the attendants: "Do whatever He tells you" (John 2:5). At this demonstration of gentle trust, Jesus could no longer resist and, having the power of determining the time of His own destiny, He anticipated that hour out of reverence for His mother.

Among the array of outstanding qualities which Mary possessed in such a high degree, we must point to the one which enshrines all others and lends them their particular charm. It is the quality of simplicity which is the touchstone of all created beauty and the most delicate flower which grows in God's garden of virtues. Associated as Mary was with her Son in His joys as well as in His trials, in His labors as well as in His passion, there is nothing which edifies us more than the simple manner in which she responded to the supernatural. Mary had been accustomed to live with God as a matter of course even before the Annunciation, and the coming of Christ in person into the little household of Nazareth did not change the order of day. It is no flight of fancy to imagine her going quietly about her menial tasks of sweeping in the morning, of planning and preparing her meals at noontime, of mending the clothing and weaving the wool when the evening shadows lengthened and night fell over the village. This lovely example of humility and simplicity is perhaps the greatest lesson Mary has left behind. It is the lesson of the hidden life of Nazareth. If we are to understand God's plans and ways as Mary did, we must know that the supernatural is not meant to make us remiss in our natural obligations. It will help us to supernaturalize the natural, which incidentally is the height of perfection. This perfection was Mary's in a superlative degree, and it was just this simplicity of Our Blessed Lady which makes her so greatly attractive and so exceedingly admirable in our eyes. It is in this sense that we understand the words of St. Grignon de Montfort: "The Most High has made Mary His treasurer and the dispenser of His favors, to ennoble, raise up, and enrich those whom she wishes to enter on the narrow way to heaven, to make them pass through the narrow gate of life in spite of difficulties. To Mary alone has God given the keys to the cellars of divine love, and the power to enter on the highest and most secret ways of perfection, which are the ways of sublime simplicity."

CHAPTER 13

MOTHER OF GOOD COUNSEL

This title received a permanent place in the Litany of Our Lady by decree of Leo XIII. It is a variation of an earlier title, "Mother of True Counsel," which is mentioned in a litany dating from the end of the thirteenth or the beginning of the fourteenth century, and found in the Library of Saint Mark's at Venice. With certain small variations, the latter conforms to the text of many contemporary manuscripts, which seems to indicate that it was already well known at that time, and that its origin goes back to an even earlier date.

The title has reference to Mary's extraordinary solicitude for the human race in her capacity of spiritual mother of mankind, and reflects directly her comprehensive knowledge of future, past, and present events in so far as they influence the temporal and spiritual welfare of her children.

As a clear concept of Mary's intellectual gifts brings us to a better understanding of her outstanding privileges as Mother of God, inspires us to love her more ardently and to seek her assistance with ever increasing confidence, we may consider the nature and degree of her knowledge under a twofold aspect: the knowledge which she possessed while still on earth, and the extent of her present knowledge in heaven. At the outset we state that there are no official pronouncements of the Church in regard to the exact nature of Mary's knowledge, but we can make use of many reasonable deductions from sound theological principles in order to arrive at a proper perspective of her outstanding mental qualities.

In attempting to determine the measure of Mary's knowledge while on earth, our first observation is that the Blessed Mother was not omniscient. Only the divine intellect is capable of knowing all things, both actual and possible. This leaves even the human nature of Christ short of this all-embracing characteristic. The human intellect of our Lord being hypostatically united to the Person of the Word possessed, however, knowledge which exceeds all human understanding, and was far superior to Mary's intelligence and corresponding knowledge. It is safe to say that Mary's intellectual gifts approached both a natural and a supernatural perfection unequalled by any other human being, since it is a general theological principle that God bestows His favors on human beings in proportion to their needs, and in accordance with the particular state and office to which each is destined.

We should distinguish between three types of knowledge within the capacity of the human mind: natural knowledge, infused knowledge, and beatific knowledge.

Natural knowledge derives its ideas from the objects perceived by the senses and is known as experimental knowledge. This knowledge is natural in the sense that it is obtained by such natural means as personal observation, instruction provided by others, reading, and the like. It is subject to gradual growth and development as new objects are perceived and additional ideas acquired with the passing of the years. Even our Lord made progress in this type of knowledge, and it could be said of Him, as we read in the Gospel, that He advanced in wisdom (Luke 2:52). As one who was destined to fulfill such an important office in the plan of redemption, Mary was undoubtedly endowed with a brilliant mind, more so, since her intellectual judgment was never dulled by sin, either original or actual. Like ours, this knowledge of Our Lady was aided and guided by faith and divine grace. Since she had fullness of grace, her faith must have been assisted by the gifts of the Holy Spirit in such a manner that she could read into the hidden meaning of revealed mysteries far deeper than even the most learned and pious Jewish scholar. She must have been particularly favored in her understanding of the mysteries of redemption, in which she herself had a part to play. The inner meaning of these mysteries, their harmony, and their consequences must have become increasingly clear to her, and she must have relished these mysteries in the measure of her growing charity, humility, and purity of heart and mind. On the other hand, we cannot accept an excessive development of knowledge in matters which did not pertain to her humble state of life, or which had no direct relation to her established vocation.

The second type of knowledge, which is directly conferred on the mind by God in the form of intellectual representations and needs no exercise of any bodily faculty, is called infused knowledge. Such knowledge was granted to the human mind of our Lord at the very moment of His Incarnation, and was undoubtedly very extensive and very profound. In Mary it was somewhat more restricted, but must have extended explicitly to the supernatural order. This knowledge must have thrown light upon the great religious and moral truths, such as the existence of God, His universal providence extending to the minutest details, the spirituality and immortality of the soul, the relation between nature and grace, free will and moral responsibility. The celebrated theologian, Father Suarez, believes that from the beginning Mary had a deep infused knowledge of the Blessed Trinity, particularly because she had been brought in such close contact with the three divine Persons; and that she had a general knowledge also of the plan of the Incarnation. She must have been aware that the Child she bore was true God, and that according to God's general design her Son was to remain in obscurity during the early years of His life on earth. This explains how she was surprised and dismayed when He left Joseph and herself to stay in Jerusalem for several days as a boy of twelve, because she apparently did not know of this exception to God's general plan. She surely did know that the accomplishment of the redemption demanded the passion and death of the Redeemer, as she was well acquainted with the Scriptures and the prophecies concerning the promised Messiah, and was able to read and interpret them in an exceptionally penetrating manner.

Among Mary's gratuitous gifts we must include that of prophecy. An example of which can be found in the *Magnificat,* when she said: "Behold, henceforth all generations shall call me blessed" (Luke 1:48). The realization of this prophecy in the course of ages is as evident as is the meaning of the words themselves. Hers was also the gift of the discernment of spirits, by which she could recognize the Spirit of God as distinguished from diabolical illusion. She could also read the secrets of hearts, all which privileges must have been hers because of her exalted selection, on the general principle that God granted Mary every grace or favor that He granted any creature, provided it was consonant with her state or vocation.

The third type of knowledge possible to the human mind, is beatific knowledge, or the knowledge which comes to a human soul which enjoys the direct perception of the divine essence. This knowledge was Christ's during His entire human career, as is confirmed by a decision of the Holy Office given in 1918. By virtue of this knowledge our Lord knew, even while on earth, all actual things, past, present, and future. He also comprehended the mysteries of science, understood all languages, knew when the day of Judgment will come, could read the thoughts of men. That Mary did not possess this kind of knowledge in the course of mortal life, at least not continuously, is evident from the fact that beatific knowledge is the explicit possession of the elect and the angels in heaven. One who enjoys the beatific vision can no longer make progress in holiness, since his state is one of stability and final consummation, and of eternal union with Divinity. Since it is established that Our Lady increased in sanctity as the years of her earthly life went on, this type of knowledge could not have been hers, at least not permanently. It may have been given her, as Suarez maintains, for brief moments at certain extraordinary events, such as the Incarnation and the actual birth of Christ at Bethlehem. This could be possible, more so, because both St. Augustine and St. Thomas hold that St. Paul at least momentarily enjoyed the beatific vision, when he was "caught up to the third heaven" (II Cor. 12:2). Both Doctors mention that, according to the Jews, the third heaven was not merely the higher atmosphere, but the spiritual heaven inhabited by

God, where He is seen face to face by the angels—paradise, as St. Paul says in the same text. Thus they conclude that St. Paul, called to be the special Doctor of grace, was probably favored by a brief moment of the beatific vision, since grace cannot be understood fully without some vision of the glory of which grace is the beginning. A similar reasoning would hold in the case of Mary. This, however, is certain, that Mary has been in possession of the beatific vision with all its glorious implications since the day of her bodily assumption into heaven.

In regard to her present knowledge we must admit the general theological principle that the knowledge of earthly events, possessed by the blessed in heaven, is measured, not by the degree of holiness to which they attained, but rather by the position in life which they occupied. Applying this norm to Mary, we must conclude that her acquaintance with earthly affairs is universal and that her ability to read the thoughts and the secrets of hearts, especially of the elect, is far greater than that of any saint, since she is the Queen of heaven and earth, and the spiritual Mother of all mankind. Her knowledge thus is determined by these exalted titles, to which we may add the present title of Mother of Good Counsel, since it is her primary office to guide her children with wisdom, and understanding, and supreme caution on their way to eternity.

CHAPTER *14*

MOTHER OF OUR CREATOR

Above the mother-and-son relationship of Mary and Jesus is Our Lady's relation to the Blessed Trinity, as its determining principle.

The external operations of the Most Holy Trinity, as the Council of Trent defines, are common to the Three Persons, although they are attributed to separate Persons according to propriety. Thus we assign to the Father, inasmuch as He is Father and the symbol of fertility, the productive power as expressed in the creation. To the Son, inasmuch as He represents God's substantial wisdom, the supreme wisdom of the work of redemption. To the Holy Spirit, inasmuch as He is the substantial love of Father and Son, the office of applying the merits of both Incarnation and redemption to the individual soul.

Apart from determining her divine maternity, the Incarnation established a union of Mary with God which differs essentially from the ordinary union of grace. It rests upon the hypostatic union of the human nature of her Son with the divine. This uniting action, which brought about the joining of the divine nature of the Eternal Word with the human nature, is ascribed to the Holy Spirit, just as the productive action of God, which brought about the God-man Jesus Christ, is expressed by the Angel as being the work of the Holy Spirit in the overshadowing of the power of the Most High. Christ, who is the Anointed of the Father, is given by the Eternal Father to the Virgin as her Son, through the influence of the Holy Spirit. By assigning, as theology does, the accomplishment of both the productive action and the unifying action to the same Holy Spirit, who Himself proceeds from the very Person who assumes humanity, it is clearly shown that the Second Person of the Blessed Trinity is absolutely complete in Himself, by virtue of the fullness of life and power which is essentially His, and which reveals itself in the Holy Spirit. Thus the union of Mary with God is not specifically limited to the Person of the Son, still less to the Father or to the Holy Spirit. It extends to the entire Trinity, as an external operation of the Godhead. On the strength of this we cannot call Mary the Mother of the Father, or of the Holy Spirit, least of all Mother of the Blessed Trinity. But we are allowed to call her Mother of the Creator with as much right as we call her the Mother of God, because she is the Mother of the incarnate Word who infused Himself, by His own creative power, in the womb of His Virgin Mother through His hypostatic infusion into the flesh taken from her, and became man.

The same consideration, which determines Our Lady's relationship with the Blessed Trinity in general and with her divine Son in particular, determines also the special cult which is accorded her in the universal Church as a distinguishing mark of our respectful deference.

Because the Blessed Virgin manifests more than any other creature the goodness and power of God, Mary cannot be treated the same as other saints. At the same time she cannot be placed on a level with our Lord, who deserves an absolute worship all His own, which is called *latria*. This term, derived from the Greek "latreia," is best translated into our language by "adoration." It is unfortunate that English does not possess the precision of the

Greek. The word *latria* is never applied in any other sense than that of the incommunicable adoration which is due to God alone. In English, the word adoration, as well as the synonymous term of worship, is sometimes used to mean also an inferior form of religious veneration. It even expresses our admiration or affection for human individuals. Those who perforce adopt these modes of expression to convey the high respect they have for persons other than God, understand perfectly well what is meant by them. The Second Council of Nicaea (787) puts the matter in few words, when it says that "true *latria* is to be given to God alone." The cult includes the sacred humanity of our Lord, as belonging to the uncreated Person of the divine Word. In a relative manner it is due also to crucifixes, and to pictures and statues which represent our Lord.

The Blessed Virgin, on the other hand, deserves more than the cult of mere respect, which is called *dulia.* This term, also derived from the Greek, indicates an inferior species of reverence, such as is due to angels and saints alike. For this reason we reserve for the Blessed Virgin a cult which is called *hyperdulia,* that is to say, *dulia* in an eminent degree. Most theologians, however, hold, that the difference between *dulia* and *hyperdulia* is one not of degree alone, but of kind as well. For, they argue, this specific cult is due Mary because she is the Mother of God. This dignity belongs by its term to the hypostatic union, and is therefore not only higher, but specifically different from the respect we owe other saints, or even angels, whose sanctity does not enter into this category.

Because of Mary's unique position in the divine economy of redemption, this cult of *hyperdulia* is so inseparable from our worship of Christ that the two cults constitute one organic whole, the one supplementing the other. This is best illustrated by the way we combine our devotion to the Holy Eucharist with our veneration of Mary, by reciting the Rosary and the Litany of Loreto while the Blessed Sacrament is exposed for our adoration. Considering the strictness with which Rome sees to it that during the exposition of the Blessed Sacrament our entire attention remains focused on the Holy Eucharist, this custom beautifully reflects the mind of the Church, which feels unable to separate the Mother from the Son. Surely Pope Pius XI recognized this fact when he granted a plenary indulgence to all those who piously recite a third part of the Rosary in the presence of the Blessed Sacrament, either publicly exposed or reserved in the tabernacle. Since the Holy Eucharist is outstandingly the sacrament of Christ's sacred humanity, we honor God most perfectly when we make Christ in His humanity the immediate object of our adoration of God. Likewise, Christ's sacred humanity is most perfectly honored when we give the person who stands closest to this humanity a place in our veneration, and make her the bearer of our adoration of Christ. The honor shown the Mother redounds at all times to the glory of the Son. For this reason, the veneration of our Blessed Mother is exercised in the Church with this specific purpose: to honor Christ more perfectly in her and by her, just as the adoration given to our Lord's humanity serves to effect a more perfect adoration of His divinity.

The cult of Mary, sanctioned by both Church and general Catholic practice, holds the middle between two extremes. On the one side is the cult of Mary which exceeds all bounds of propriety by placing her on a level with our Lord, and can best be described by the term Mariolatry. On the other side is the lack of due respect for Our Lady, as if honor shown to Mary reflects on the absolute honor and worship which is due to Christ alone. While the Protestant attitude seems to accuse us of the first extreme, they themselves have lapsed into the second. The proper procedure is to keep to the middle of the road. Catholics well realize that Mary is only a reflection of the divine munificence as expressed in Christ, and a better knowledge of Mary will result in a deeper understanding of God. No one deprives the Son of honor when due respect is paid to the Mother. In conclusion we remark that experience shows that faith in the divinity of Christ has best been preserved in those countries which are marked by a special devotion to the Blessed Mother. Nor has the Church ever produced a saint who was not deeply devoted to both Jesus and Mary.

CHAPTER 15

MOTHER OF OUR SAVIOR

When we name Mary Mother of our Savior, we wish to express as a first consideration that God, through Mary, presented the world with the Redeemer. Second, it brings to the fore Mary's personal activity in the work of the redemption. This need not cause any misgiving as to the possibility of depriving Christ of the explicit and full credit which is His due. Mary was redeemed herself, and her power to cooperate in such an exalted task was entirely determined by and dependent on God's own eternal decree. Still, there was a formal cooperation on the part of Mary. We may even designate it as a cooperating partnership in the execution of the work of redemption, called for and accepted by our Lord, not in order to achieve or complete the intrinsic power of the redeeming work, but rather to perfect its beauty and loveliness. Here the words of St. Bernard are relevant. "It is true," the Saint says, "that Christ alone would have been adequate to bring about redemption, since all our sufficiency is from Him. But it was more appropriate that Jesus and Mary should work together. Jesus Christ as man obviously is the trustworthy mediator between God and man, but mankind honors in Him His majesty. Not only His mercy, but also His judgment is sung. There is thus need of a human mediator, next to the divine, and none could be more fitting than Mary."

In keeping with the preceding quotation Mary has been called not simply a cooperating partner in the redemption, but a co-redeeming partner, or, to use the accepted term, Co-redemptrix. From the sixteenth century on, sporadically at first, but with ever increasing impetus, this term has been used. When we keep clearly in mind that the word does not aim to express coordinated principles, but that it has only and sole reference to Mary's ministerial subordination, we may use it without danger. At any rate, the term has the official sanction of the highest ecclesiastical circles of later date, such as the Sacred Congregation of Rites, which calls Mary the "compassionate Co-redemptrix of the human race" (May 13, 1908). Blessed Pope Pius X granted an indulgence to an Italian prayer which uses a similar expression. Benedict XV and Pius XI both added their authority to the orthodoxy of the term in question. The title, therefore, will stand, regardless of the objections raised by Protestants, for the good reason that it has cost Our Lady, who bears it, so many and such painful sacrifices.

What is the precise extent of Mary's cooperation in the work of Christ's redemption?

Mary took a long time preparing for this exalted task. It began with a remote and moral preparation before conception. As such, it coincided with the general preparation by which all men had to ready themselves for the reception of the grace of redemption. It combined a pious longing for the Redeemer with a sincere desire to do all within their power to obtain this redeeming grace. On the part of Mary, although unwittingly, it consisted in preparing a worthy dwelling place for the Redeemer within herself, and in the human race. In this operation she was aided by her perfect disposition to do God's holy will in every respect. Because of the fullness of grace which had been hers from the first moment of her conception, she was preserved not only from all stain of sin, but also from any inclination to deviate from God's directives. At the same time, by the power of the Holy Spirit working in her, she could worthily obtain from God the sending of the Redeemer, not by way of reward in justice, but as an effect of her prayerful entreaties which were made efficacious by her state of special friendship with God. The Fathers indicate this form of Mary's cooperation when they say that, by her perfect disposition she made the Son of God descend into her womb.

In the act of conceiving her Son as the Redeemer of the human race, Mary cooperated directly and effectively by giving her explicit consent. This consent was not merely given in respect to the use of her maternal activity in its instrumental working of nature. It was a voluntary accept-

ance of her part in the work of redemption. Since her Son
was announced to her as the Redeemer of the world, her
consent was formally given in order to make the redemption possible. This is the way the Fathers explain it. They
maintain that Mary's consent was an eminently moral act,
which implied objectively and directly a true dependence
of the work of redemption on her will. Since this dependence was willed and arranged for by God Himself, it was
such that it by no means exposed God's plan of redemption
to the danger of frustration. Together with that eternal decree, God provided also the assurance of Mary's consent.

After conception, Mary's moral cooperation continued
uninterruptedly. During her entire life she remained conscious of the role she was to play in the mystery drama of
her divine Son. She knew that to be a mother meant suffering. She also knew that to be the mother of the Savior
meant suffering in extreme proportion. Ever since the
prophet Simeon had acquainted her with the fact that a
sword of grief would pierce her soul, she had realized that
this Child, who was destined for the fall and the rise of
many in Israel, could not save the world without blood.
Here the words of Blessed Pope Pius X are significant, who
says: "Mary's community of life and sufferings with her Son
was never broken off. To her as to Him may be applied the
words of the prophet, 'My life is wasted away with grief,
and my days in sighs.' She accepted the mission of protecting and nourishing the Lamb of sacrifice, and, when the
time came, led Him to the altar of immolation." When she
met our Lord on the way to Calvary, Mary knew that He
was led as a sheep to the slaughter, and the Cross which He
carried, and the drops of blood which marked the way were
the price of redemption.

Beneath the Cross, Mary's cooperation assumed its highest form and reached its true completion. By offering her Son to the Father as a sacrifice of propitiation for the sins of the world, her cooperation was indeed actual and personal. In this respect an anonymous author of the twelfth century remarks: "There was one will and one sacrifice in Mother and Son: the one in the blood of Mary's heart, the other in the blood of our Lord's body." Nor did Mary's sacrifice lack its own share of effectiveness. Although it does not add to the intrinsic power of the redeeming sacrifice of her Son, it cannot for that reason be considered purely ornamental and accidental. According to God's eternal decree Mary's sacrifice added something to the substantial integrity of her Son's, inasmuch as Christ desired as little to act apart from and without her, as she can act apart from and without Him. For this reason, and in this sense, the effects of our Lord's sacrifice must be regarded as conjointly obtained by Jesus and Mary, and we may say that by her cooperation with Christ, she gave satisfaction to God for sin, merited grace, and redeemed the world, always in and through Jesus Christ. In this manner we may also consider Mary as a contributing cause to the fruits of the redemption, as St. Cyril of Alexandria says so beautifully: "Hail Mary, Mother of God, who art to be venerated as the treasure of the whole world. By whom the Blessed Trinity is adored and glorified, the redeeming Cross is venerated; by whom the angels and archangels rejoice, the devils take to flight, the diabolical tempter falls from heaven; by whom the fallen are taken up; by whom every human creature is brought to the knowledge of the truth; by whom holy baptism and the oil of exultation reach the faithful; by whom churches are established the world over; by whom nations are brought to penance; by whom the only-begotten Son of God for ages past has enlightened those who were sitting in darkness and in the shadow of death."

Summarizing this final cooperation of Mary beneath the Cross, Bossuet remarks: "Mary gave birth to Jesus without pain; but she brings forth the faithful in most cruel suffering. At what price has she bought them! They have cost her her only Son. She can be Mother of Christians only by giving her Son to death. O agonizing fruitfulness! It was the will of the Eternal Father that the adoptive sons should be born by the death of the true Son. United to the Eternal Father she must offer His Son and hers to die on the Cross. It was for that purpose that Providence brought her to the foot of the Cross."

CHAPTER 16

VIRGIN MOST PRUDENT

As a postscript to the preceding chapter and by way of corollary, we may point to the depth of Mary's faith, hope, and charity, while standing beneath the Cross. Since she was ignorant of the detailed plans of God's wisdom regarding the work of redemption, Mary's faith was tested to the utmost in this mournful hour. It is easy to believe in Christ as the Savior in the face of achievement. But when years of thoughtful and patient effort were swept away before the powers of evil, when hope turned into despondency, success into failure, light into darkness, it took more than a Mother's faith in her Son to keep trust with God. Father Garrigou-Lagrange holds that Mary's act of faith at this moment was the greatest ever elicited by any human being. Her faith never wavered when Jesus seemed completely vanquished and His work annihilated. Regardless of all evidence to the contrary she understood that when Jesus uttered His last words the work of salvation had been accomplished, according to God's unfailing plan.

Calvary also witnessed her supreme act of hope at the moment when everything appeared so futile and so utterly lost. While her Son's answer to the good thief, who asked to be remembered when Christ had entered into His kingdom, may have seemed to others a simple word of kindness, to Mary it was more than a gentle reassurance. It was a promise that Paradise was about to be opened to receive this man and all the elect who would ask to be remembered in days to come.

Unselfish charity was represented on Calvary, next to our Lord's, when Mary offered her Son under such heart-rending circumstances, that others would live. Nor would her faith and hope have been able to reveal such particular splendor, had not charity enlivened them with its own particular charm. There is an intrinsic relationship and a mutual dependency of all virtues, their degree of efficiency being gauged by the measure of charity. But even charity is dependent on one of its subordinate virtues, and finds its final term in the virtue of prudence.

The word prudence—a contraction of providence—indicates a tendency to look ahead. It is an intellectual habit which enables a person to determine, in any given circumstance, what is virtuous and therefore desirable, and what is not; it shows the mind the correct way to arrive at the one and avoid the other. Prudence makes no distinction in respect to theological or moral virtues in its directive activity; it presides over the production of all acts proper to each virtue, and is the universal guiding star which gives direction to all. While prudence thus aims at perfecting not the will but the intellect, and is directly concerned with determining the course of action to be taken, it does not neglect to provide the directive principle of the moral action, and is rightly called a moral virtue. Next to this virtue of prudence, there is a corresponding gift of the Holy Spirit, the gift of counsel. This gift provides a person with prompt and right judgment, not by careful search of the mind, but by way of supernatural intuition. St. Thomas remarks that, in his search of guidance man has to be directed by God. It is the Spirit of counsel which makes us wise in the ways of God.

While Our Lady's behavior at the Annunciation bespeaks her faith and humility and her readiness to do God's will, it also gives evidence of her supreme prudence. Pondering within herself what the salutation of the Angel augured, Mary kept her peace, and awaited further details from the mouth of Gabriel.

"And the Angel said to her: 'Do not be afraid, Mary, for thou hast found grace with God. And behold, thou shalt conceive in thy womb and shalt bring forth a son; and thou shalt call his name Jesus. He shall be great, and shall be called the son of the Most High; and the Lord God will give him the throne of David his father, and he shall be king over the house of Jacob forever; and of his kingdom there shall be no end' " (Luke 1:30–33).

Even this explanation left Mary uncertain as to the nature of the promised child. Was it not possible that the Angel spoke of an eminently prominent, earthly king? Thus, not desiring to go against the words of Gabriel, which were evidently God's own, she inquired cautiously how this should happen, since she did not know man.

"And the Angel answered and said to her: 'The Holy Spirit shall come upon thee and the power of the Most High shall overshadow thee; and therefore the Holy One to be born shall be called the Son of God' " (Luke 1:35).

It was then that all doubts concerning her selection as the mother of the Messiah were removed, and Mary spoke her classic answer: "Behold the handmaid of the Lord; be it done to me according to thy word" (Luke 1:38).

Another illustration of Our Lady's supreme prudence is recorded in St. Matthew. "When Mary had been betrothed to Joseph, she was found, before they came together, to be with child" (Matt. 1:18). Rather than take it upon herself to explain to Joseph and reveal the secrets of God, she entrusted her state of perplexity to God, who sent an angel to reassure Joseph.

Instead of claiming her right of exemption, she did what every other Jewish woman was obliged to do after childbirth, and presented herself in the Temple to be purified, thus avoiding undue prominence to herself and her Child. A similar supernatural providence, perhaps with a bit of human touch, was exhibited by Mary at the marriage feast at Cana, when her discreet insistence—"Do whatever He tells you" (John 2:5)—brought about the first miracle of our Lord.

A final example may be drawn from Our Lady following her Son to Calvary. She was well aware that it was her Son's sacrifice; that He was to tread the winepress alone (Is. 63:3). Still she felt that her presence at that fatal hour was most urgent. As the Mother of the Redeemer, her place was beneath the Cross. Who would deny that all this was done under the direct inspiration of the Holy Spirit, who wished Mary to complete her own sacrifice and share in the sacrifice of her Son.

These are but a few scattered examples. The Gospel is sparing with revealing details of Mary's hidden life, but to believe that she was under the continual direction of the Holy Spirit in this respect, is only an inference from her fullness of grace.

In our restless search to know the things of God and to act according to His eternal designs, we feel the urgent need of this gift of prudence. "Without it," says Father Saint Jure, "there is confusion of thought, lack of reflection, blindness in designs, hastiness in resolutions, presumption and precipitation in action." Left to our own devices, we are like those who sow a wind and reap a whirlwind. Well may we turn to Our Blessed Lady under her present title, and assure ourselves of that supernatural guidance which was hers throughout her life, and will be ours in due measure through her powerful intercession.

CHAPTER 17

VIRGIN MOST VENERABLE

Anyone who tries to sing the praises of Mary, even on a modest scale, must feel disheartened to find her name so little mentioned in the New Testament. Since Our Blessed Lady was most venerable and worthy of reverence, it seems surprising that neither our Lord, nor the Apostles or the Evangelists, endeavored to throw greater light upon the glory of Mary, other than naming her the Mother of Jesus. The usual reason given for this apparent neglect is that our Lord's glory and His personal eminence had to be established first, before there could be any question of the glory of the Mother. At the same time it is obvious that during Mary's lifetime her humility was to be respected, shielded, and safeguarded. We may perhaps search a little deeper and find some light in the relationship of Jesus and Mary, which was not of the same kind as is the ordinary relationship of a man and his mother. The true meaning of Mary's motherhood was a divine motherhood, and any too human and carnal idea of this relationship was to be discouraged at any cost. This reason received prominence when, during the exercise of His ministry, our Lord was approached by His mother in the company of some relatives who wished to speak to Him. Instead of granting their request without delay, our Lord replied to those who informed Him, that His Mother and His brethren were those who hear the word of God and act upon it (Luke 8:21). In a similar manner Jesus made response to the woman who blessed the womb that bore Him, when He said: "Rather, blessed are they who hear the word of God and keep it" (Luke 11:28). Nothing was farther from His mind than to slight His mother on either occasion. It was rather that Christ wished to emphasize the supernatural side of His mission and the true character of the relationship between Him and His mother. For, it was precisely by hearing the word of God and acting upon it, that Mary became the Mother of the Redeemer. "Blessed is she who has believed, because the things promised her by the Lord shall be accomplished" (Luke 1:45).

It bears remembering also, that Jesus implied nothing derogatory when He addressed Our Lady on two occasions by the word "woman." In formal address this word expresses high respect in the language spoken by Jesus, which is strikingly indicated when He used it on the Cross:

"Woman, behold thy son" (John 19:26). The latter instance indicated the unusual concern our Lord felt for His Mother whom He looked upon, on this occasion more than ever, as the worthy Mother of all men. A similar explanation fits the words which He spoke at the wedding feast at Cana: "What wouldst thou have Me do, woman? My hour has not yet come" (John 2:4). Rather than saying that our Lord withdrew Himself from the law of filial obedience to Mary as the Son of God, we prefer to view the situation from the solemn implication it involved, namely, that Jesus was prompted to advance the time of His first miracle because of Mary. Here was demonstrated more than ever the high regard which He had for His Mother; and the eminent dignity of the divine maternity is revealed to us in a new light, honored by tradition, that of "omnipotentia supplex," omnipotence in the order of supplication.

This latter characteristic of Mary continues today through her maternal intercession in the order of grace. It is this maternal note which distinguishes her intercession from that of the saints, who intercede as friends and servants of the Bridegroom. While in heaven the glory of Mary's Son is in absolute evidence, the glory of Mary is founded upon the sacred humanity of Jesus Christ. Because heavenly bliss and glory are proportioned to the degree of grace and charity which precedes entry there, it is theologically certain that Mary's essential beatitude surpasses both in intensity and extension the beatitude and the corresponding honor conferred on all the other blessed. It is also theologically established that even Mary's initial fullness of grace surpassed the final grace of the highest saints and angels, inasmuch as this fullness is the fruit of Mary's relationship to the hypostatic union of her Son with the divine Word. This implies that Mary's beatific vision penetrates more deeply into the divine essence seen face to face than that of all other blessed. Mary's heavenly glory is second only to the splendor of her divine Son, and consequently is so intensive that we do not hesitate to say with St. Albert the Great that she constitutes, among the blessed, an order apart.

On the other hand Mary's intercession remains distinguished from that of the Bridegroom Himself, who lives to make intercession for us at the right hand of God (Rom. 8:34). Mary shares in her Son's divine activity of salvation today in the same measure that she cooperated with Him while on earth, in obtaining the grace of redemption. Her power and dignity are based on the sublime and proper power and dignity of her Son, which in turn is expressed in His full spiritual fatherhood over mankind. Mary is subordinate to this as much as any creature, for which reason she pleads and petitions for all that she desires in and by her Son. This intercession, directed to Christ Himself, is explained by the services which she alone rendered to His person. In this connection the Greek Fathers applied to Mary the title of Advocate, an expression used almost exclusively of her and not of the saints. It is the name which Sacred Scripture assigns to the Holy Spirit, and contains a special consecration. It is particularly appropriate to Mary since, by reason of her special relationship, the Holy Spirit unites Himself to her petitions before her Son.

In the face of these several honors bestowed upon Mary, the Church has called her Virgin Most Venerable. All these prerogatives are only a reflection of her exalted position as Mother of Christ, the Savior, since the same all-embracing grace which explains Mary's unique place in the economy of the redemption, also determines her eminent dignity and her present glory.

CHAPTER 18

VIRGIN MOST RENOWNED

In the consideration of the present glory of Mary in the preceding chapter we established the fact that her glory and dignity are a direct result of her divine maternity. In view of the great variety of extraordinary graces which were given to her in virtue of this selection, combined with the numberless implications this selection involved, we were unable so far to give much thought to the foundation of Mary's singular privilege, in order to determine the real essence of this mystery. Still, this relationship of Mary with her divine Son is the keynote of her most glorious position within God's creation, and the basis of the entire Mariology.

In order to determine the specific character of this relationship, it is not enough to consider Our Lady's motherhood as an office given by God, the worthy execution of which needed to be made possible and rewarded by special graces. Nor is it sufficient to consider the bodily relationship of Mary and Jesus as a privilege analogous to the one every mother acquires because she gave life to the fruit of her womb. The real relationship between our Lord and the Blessed Mother goes much deeper. It is, in reality, a supernatural, spiritual union of the person of Mary with that of her Son. This union cannot be set forth more simply or clearly, or with more regard to reality than through the expression of a divine marriage, and that in the strictest sense of the word. It is a relation which, with regard to God, forms the highest and most complete association possible between a created person and Himself, just as human marriage is the highest and most perfect union possible between two persons. In accordance with the nature of marriage, this union includes a solidarity of both persons in an organic whole, in which they have grown together in mutual possession. The divine Word, as infused and implanted in His Virgin Mother, gives Himself to her and takes her to Himself as partner and helper, in the closest, strictest, and most lasting community of life, in such a manner that henceforth there is but one mind and one purpose and one field of action. In the supernatural order there cannot exist another relationship which could bring a created person—in this instance the Blessed Virgin—closer to God than this divine union through which she is organically united with God.

That this idea of a divine marriage is not strange to the teachings of the Church is evident from the fact that, in the common supernatural order, the highest union possible between God and the soul is designated by the name of spiritual marriage. This mystic union, however, which finds its foundation in sanctifying grace, is far inferior to the union which the divine Word effected with His Virgin Mother, inasmuch as the latter enjoyed the double privilege of a physical and a spiritual union, while the former is exclusively spiritual.

We find an analogy of this divine marriage in the mystery of the hypostatic union, which itself is defined as a marriage between the divine and the human nature. As previously mentioned, both the productive and the uniting action of this hypostatic union are ascribed to the Holy Spirit. But, all the while this specific operation which produced the Incarnation may be attributed in all propriety to the Son alone who, during this operation, and after, as well as before, remained substantially united to the Father and the Holy Spirit in the unity of nature. For the Person who assumed humanity is absolutely complete in Himself, and assumes the flesh by virtue of His fullness of life and power, which reveals itself in the Holy Spirit. When Jesus received His humanity from His Virgin Mother, Mary became the link between the human race and the Godhead which made this marriage of the divine and human possible, and the full analogy of the divine marriage of Jesus and Mary is complete in the hypostatic union, even to the productive action, for it brought about the existence of Christ, the Anointed of the Father, even as the divine Word, infusing Himself in the womb of His Virgin Mother, brought about the God-man Jesus, the Redeemer of the world.

This extraordinary, supernatural prerogative of grace, which is Mary's exclusive privilege, and which received its completion at the moment when the divine Word infused Himself in her and made her His Mother, presupposes a prior spiritual union in and through which it was perfected. This preceding union cannot be understood as a simple, friendly union such as is effected by habitual grace. It must have been a very special grace, achieved through the will of the Creator, through which the divine Word was already appropriated by right to the Virgin, and by which He was spiritually united to her in preparation for the day of conception. With this readiness and under this form, the grace of motherhood was granted to her in a natural way.

In addition we must observe that this grace of Mary's maternity was a free gift of God and could not be merited in any form. It concerned a union with God which does not belong to the common order of habitual grace but has a direct relation to the hypostatic union, inasmuch as it aimed to cooperate in, and actually effect the personal union of the humanity of Jesus to the uncreated Word, through the joint instrumentality of Mary and the Holy Spirit. The fact that it was decreed by God from all eternity leaves indeed little room for any acquiring or disposing activity on the part of Mary to make this grace possible. The words of St. Thomas must be understood in this sense, when he says: "The Blessed Virgin is said to have merited to bear the Lord of all, not because she merited His becoming man, but because through grace given her she merited such a degree of purity and sanctity that she could fittingly be the Mother of God." In this manner it was an entirely free gift of God, one which was exclusively prepared for Mary.

That this preparatory, spiritual union between the divine Word and His Mother-to-be actually existed, both in this form and for this particular purpose, may be inferred from the words of Pius IX, who states that by one and the same decree God prescribed the origin of the Blessed Virgin and the Incarnation of divine Wisdom. This is further emphasized by God's own words, spoken in Paradise centuries before the actual birth of Mary, in which He declared His intention to crush Satan's head by the joint operation of the Woman and her seed, in contradistinction to the joint operation of Adam and Eve, which had caused spiritual ruin to mankind.

Looking thus at the double mystery of Mary's divine conception and the hypostatic union, we discover not only an analogy of the two operations but a real interdependence. Because of this intrinsic relation of the two mysteries, we may truthfully say that Mary's grace of maternity was of the hypostatic order, and that she was created entirely in and for this union with the divine Word, even as the humanity of Christ is created entirely in and for the hypostatic union. It is finally because of this unique privilege, which underlies the mystery of the divine maternity and forms its very essence, that we give glory to Mary in such a special way, and add to her previous titles this present glorious title of Virgin Most Renowned.

CHAPTER 19

VIRGIN MOST POWERFUL

In the attempt to describe the extent of Mary's power we should recall the preceding doctrine of her divine maternity, which forms, as it were, the nucleus of all her supernatural prerogatives. In all its unique glory the grace of maternity made Mary a person of supernatural nature or order and, as such, defined her proper existence. By reason of this grace she became the bodily dwelling place of uncreated Grace, and appears next to, with, and immediately after Christ in such an eminent way that the Church does not hesitate to apply to her the spiritual descriptions which fit Eternal Wisdom, as she does to Christ Himself. Where our Lord is called the Son of the Eternal Father, Mary is called, in contrast with all other creatures, the only and the first-born daughter of God. The *only born*— because her particular grace cannot be found in any other creature; the *first-born*—because Mary is not only the first in rank among the children of God, but also the mother of all others. Analogous also to eternal Wisdom, Mary is the first-born of the entire creation, for in God's decree she is intended, with incarnate Wisdom, to be the end and the glorious completion of all the works of God. Before time was made and before all ages, Mary was in God's mind, even when the Father brought forth uncreated Wisdom within His bosom, since it was determined from all eternity that uncreated Wisdom would become man through the instrumentality of Mary.

While the Church thus transfers several attributes of eternal Wisdom to Mary, it likewise appropriates the name of Lord, designating the Son, to the Virgin Mother and, following her gracious example, we address Mary as *Our Lady*. Because this title is granted to the Mother of God in and with the person of her Son, it also includes the right of joint disposal of the goods of God. For, next to God and Christ Mary is the secondary principle of grace, and thus constitutes a supernatural complement to Christ, particularly in this respect. This gives her a unique status in the economy of grace for, while toward Christ she stands with the rest of mankind as a natural being, dependent on the influence of grace, at the side of Christ she appears as a supernatural being above other men, distributing the graces of her Son. This she does with strict right, because she communicated the first principle of grace to the world, after it was appropriated in a singularly unique manner to herself. Thus, along with other privileges, this title implies the right to submissive veneration and humble obedience from all creatures who depend on God.

The glory and power of Mary find lasting expression in the figure of the Apocalypse, where she is represented as "the woman clothed with the sun" (Apoc. 12:1). Although this prophecy prefigures the Church of the Old and the

New Covenants, which must bring forth Christ to the world, it has, from time immemorial, been applied to our Blessed Mother. Significant in this connection are the words of St. Bernard, who says: "By right Mary is called the one clothed with the sun, the one who penetrated beyond the deepest abyss of divine Wisdom, so that, as much as such a position is permitted to a creature without a personal union, she seems immersed in that inaccessible light." It is quite evident that the Liturgy would apply these words to Mary, since she is the prototype of the Church, which is the Bride of Christ and the spiritual Mother of all Christians. As such the Church stands between Christ and His spiritual children, having arisen herself from the side of Christ, and forming a helper which assists Him. As a supernatural principle of grace, the Church also finds its prototype in the supernatural, distinguishing mark of Mary, and is animated by the Spirit of Christ, which is the Holy Spirit. For the Church has a supernatural essence and existence only in so far as the Holy Spirit is her Spirit and completes her in Himself. Thus, Mary, animated by the Holy Spirit in her entire being, brings forth Jesus Christ, in which manner the idea of the Church as a supernatural principle of grace assisting Christ at once obtains its full, concrete, and living figure. Mary's personal position in the internal organism of the Church is so strikingly characteristic that we often go to her instead of turning to Christ, knowing full well that in her is the fullness of power according to her eternal position within the Church. That this is in full keeping with the spirit of the Church is well illustrated by her general practice. For the Church realizes that Jesus Himself wishes that we should have recourse to Mary so that our prayers may have greater value when they are presented by her. Theology explains this general practice of the faithful by pointing to two fundamental reasons for Mary's power of intercession.

Since she is the Mother of men, Mary knows their needs, as was mentioned before when we treated of Mary's universal knowledge. It is a general principle, admitted by all theologians, that the happiness of the blessed in heaven would not be complete if they did not know what happens on earth, at least in the matter of what concerns them by reason of their office, or their special relations with men. Such knowledge is the object of a legitimate desire, and with all the more reason, when the knowledge the blessed desire is of men's spiritual needs, and is therefore desired in charity. Fathers and mothers who have departed this life, know the needs of their children, especially those which bear on their salvation. The same may be said of the founders of religious institutes. With all the more reason may we say the same of Our Lady, who, as Mother of all men, was commissioned to sponsor the spiritual life of all, to give and to nourish it.

Knowing our spiritual needs, and even the temporal needs which have a bearing on our salvation, Mary is obviously impelled by her great charity to intercede for us. There is no question here of her acquiring new merits in heaven, but simply of obtaining that her merits, and those of her Son, be applied to us at the proper time. Standing as she does between other creatures and God, her power of intercession is most efficient, for she is not merely close to God, but, in virtue of her divine motherhood, she forms a substantial and organic link which puts creation in direct contact with God.

Mary's universal motherhood, with all the power it embodies, is often explained in a one-sided manner, especially when it is made to derive exclusively from her bodily motherhood in regard to Christ. In this way it assumes the character of a merely adoptive motherhood, a relation which could be achieved apart from Mary's physical motherhood of Christ. The essence of Mary's universal motherhood is grasped more closely when we see it as an extension of the relationship which exists between her and her Son on the one hand, and those children who proceed from this union on the other. Thus the second motherhood is achieved through the first, and shares the nature of the first so much that it rises above the idea of a merely adoptive motherhood. This point of view was in the minds of the Fathers when they based Mary's universal motherhood on the fact that she brought forth in Christ the Head of all mankind. While her motherhood is thus broadened, there still remains the difference between a natural and a spiritual motherhood. Pointing to this, St. Augustine says: "Physically, Mary is the mother of Christ only; spiritually, she is the mother of us, His members." Indeed, our spiritual relationship with Mary is conditioned by the supernatural character of her twofold motherhood. She thus acquires her power over us from the power which inheres in her dominion over the children of her Son. This dominative power explains at once her extraordinary intercessory influence in respect to us, whom she conceived as her children in and with Christ, our Lord.

CHAPTER 20

VIRGIN MOST MERCIFUL

Virgin Most Merciful is one of Mary's most charming titles. Mercy is a virtue of the will and, as St. Thomas notes, it is the virtue of the powerful and the good, who are capable of giving real assistance. It is found in God especially, as one of the prayers of the Missal has it: "O God, who dost manifest the glory of Thy power more than ever in sparing and showing mercy." In this respect St. Augustine remarks that it is more glorious for God to obtain good out of evil than to create out of nothing. He says: "It is greater to convert a sinner by giving him grace than to make a whole universe, heaven and earth included."

The virtue of mercy is found also in Mary in an extraordinary degree and, next to begetting the Author of grace, it remains Mary's greatest glory that she makes grace available to the pitiful sinner. But she also gives grace to her spiritual children in general. Even during her life Mary distributed graces in a manner so unobtrusive that it nearly passed unnoticed. St. John the Baptist was sanctified in the womb of his mother by the simple fact of Mary's appearance in the home of Elizabeth. The faith of our Lord's disciples found confirmation at His first miracle at Cana at her request. She was instrumental in bringing the Holy Spirit upon the apostles, when she prayed with them in the Cenacle of the Last Supper in preparation for the light and strength and grace of Pentecost (Acts 1:14). Christ as the Redeemer of the human race was not given to the world without her cooperation, and His redeeming power stays inseparably bound up with her. This brings up the question of Mary's universal mediation and the manner in which she distributes the graces which are placed at her disposal.

When we speak of Mary's universal mediation, her subordination to the mediation of Jesus Christ must be established as a first principle. There is an essential difference between the two. Mary's is rather an intermediate position inasmuch as she mediates with Christ, and in Christ with God; while our Lord is at once the first principle and the last end of man's union with God. This distinction stands out more clearly when we say that our Lord, in His person of incarnate God, brings men closer to the Deity as the direct bearer and representative of the influence of God on creatures. Mary, on the contrary, appears as the first among men to whom God approaches and whom He unites to Himself in Christ, because she received the communication of God first and most directly.

A second principle of no less importance concerns the joined merits of our Lord and His Blessed Mother. Although Mary's merits are joined to those of her Son, they do not add any necessary complement to the merits of our Lord, which are superabundant and sufficient in themselves. This does not eliminate, but rather underlines the fact that Mary, by her cooperation in the redeeming sacrifice of her Son, became an integral part of that sacrifice, and that her cooperation was so directed and disposed by God Himself as to make His sacrifice, through her cooperation, a complete sacrifice for mankind. In consequence of this it must be said that only in and through Mary did mankind come into possession of Christ's sacrificial merits. Mary is thus the depositary of Christ's merits since, in her particular way, she shared in obtaining them, and by God's unchangeable decree has charge of distributing them.

This doctrine is theologically certain. It has been a part of the Church's teachings for many centuries and has been confirmed by the encyclicals of several Supreme Pontiffs. Bossuet summarizes this doctrine in his sermon on the compassion of Our Lady, where he says: "O Most Blessed Virgin Mary, you have in your hands the key that opens the treasures of divine blessings. That key is your Son. He closes, and no one can open; He opens, and no one can close. It is His innocent blood which makes us to be inundated with heavenly graces. To whom will He give the right to that blood, if not to her from whom He drew it." This traditional doctrine, thus formulated by Bossuet, was proclaimed by Leo XIII in his first encyclical on the Rosary, in which he calls Mary "the dispenser of heavenly graces." In a following encyclical on the same subject, he makes the absolute claim that "no grace is given to us except through Mary, such being the divine will." He makes his own the words of St. Bernard and calls Mary our Mediatrix, and concludes with the famous words that "no one can come to the Father except by the Son, in much the same manner as no one can come to the Son except by Mary." Pius X calls Mary "the dispensatrix of all the graces which Jesus acquired for us by His blood." Benedict XV gave the doctrine his formal sanction when he instituted the feast of "Our Lady, Mediatrix of All Graces," and ordained its universal observance on May 31. In view of this general approval of the ordinary teaching power of the Church, the consensus of theologians, and the final approbation of the Liturgy, it seems that this doctrine of Mary's universal mediation can be defined as a dogma of faith. It is at least implicitly revealed in the several titles which tradition bestows on Mary—of which the Litany of Loreto is a fair example—and, although not yet dogmatically established, it may be safely used for devotional purposes.

A few explanations of the doctrine in question seem in order here. First, the universality of Mary's mediation does not imply that we need ask her explicitly for all the graces of which we stand in need. It does denote, however, that Mary actually supplies all the graces which we receive, because of our implicit intention to ask for them in the manner and according to the order established by divine providence.

It may also be noted that Mary's mediation is essentially different from that of the saints. The latter can do nothing in the form of mediation without Mary's intercession, for the very reason that her mediation is universal. Her mediation is also one of strict right, since it is founded upon her divine maternity. In union with Christ Mary has merited all the graces which she distributes, while the saints often obtain graces which they themselves did not merit. Mary's intercession has often been called an omnipotence of intercession, resting as it does on the merits of Jesus Christ and on our Lord's love for His Mother. This does not obscure His own intercession before the throne of God. On the contrary, it is one of our Lord's most divine manifestations of efficiency and delicate mercy to allow Mary to intercede for us before Him with such efficacy, since we can approach her with the confidence of a child approaching his mother.

We now inquire as to the manner in which Mary exercises her unique prerogative of Mediatrix of all graces. It is evident that the actions of the Mother of God are objectively marks of honor and service toward God. At the same time, they are actions which are endowed with the specific characteristics of her own personality, such as first-born daughter of the Father, Bride of Christ, and chosen instrument of the Holy Spirit. As such, Mary's intercession is eminently holy and exceedingly pleasing to God, and enriched with an authority which, in a sense, is delegated and given to her actions by God Himself. It is evident also that the entire supernatural activity to which Mary is called by virtue of the grace of her motherhood, can be exercised only in dependence on and in union with that of Christ. Still, the community of power between Christ and Mary is so close and so all-embracing that nowhere on earth can a perfect likeness of it be found in the cooperation of any two persons. It can be better understood and properly valued by the supernatural prototype which it has in the community of action of Christ and His Church. With this in mind, we quote the words of Father Bernard, who describes the method employed by God to distribute His graces through Mary. "God and His Christ make use of Mary by letting all graces which They destine for us pass through her. By using her as an intermediary, They temper Their action all the more with humanity, without in any way diminishing its efficacy. They make Mary live by the life by which They Themselves live, and by which we are to live. She is first filled to overflowing with it, since grace is pre-formed in her and receives in her the imprint of special beauty. All graces come to us thus canalized and distributed by her, impregnated with that delicate sweetness which she imparts to all she touches and all she does. Like the Church, Mary enters into our lives as bearer of the divine. In the whole course of our lives: from the cradle and before it, to the grave and beyond it, there is nothing of grace in which she has no part. She shapes us to the likeness of her

Son. She leaves her mark on everything and adds to the perfection of what passes through her hands. We are sustained by her prayer; we are similarly sustained by her action and, if one may say it, have our spiritual being in her."

As a whole Mary's influence on our souls remains shrouded in mystery, the same mystery which enshrines her divine maternity. But, even though the manner of Mary's action remains hidden from us on this side of the grave, the fact of her influence is in no way doubtful. After all is said, it may be best explained as a result of her spiritual motherhood and as an effect of her unique position in the economy of God's design, which is analogous to the position of a mother in the natural community of the family. This may explain in part why her mediation takes on the form of mercy rather than of justice, and we add to her previous title of Virgin Most Powerful this glorious title of Virgin Most Merciful.

CHAPTER 21

VIRGIN MOST FAITHFUL

When in the preceding chapter we spoke of Mary's universal mediation and placed special emphasis on her mercy in regard to sinners, we did not overlook the evident fact that her mediation concerns itself particularly with the work of sanctification. Even in her activity of bringing souls back to her Son, Mary's principal objective is to get them started once again on the road to perfection. It is a

consoling observation that, after God has made use of
Mary to bring about the Incarnation of His Son, He continues to make use of her in the sanctification of souls.
To this charge Mary has been ever faithful, since it has to
do with the actual continuation of the Incarnation of her
Son, by which He is spiritually born again in souls. This
work of sanctifying individuals also particularly concerns
Mary in as far as it is an extension of the work of the Holy
Spirit, which was so wonderfully begun in her from the
first moment of her conception; came to its climax when
the same Holy Spirit overshadowed her; and finds its final
glory when she communicates to us that same supernatural
life of grace as a gift of the Holy Spirit, and fosters its continual growth.

How Mary influences souls to lead them to an ever-
increasing intimacy with our Blessed Lord is a pertinent
question, which deserves a somewhat closer scrutiny. There
is no denying the fact that our present day has been called
the age of Mary. And not without reason. In view of her
God-given prerogative as Mother of the Redeemer, and
because of the influence which she has on the heart of her
Son, she has set out in her own inimitable way to retain
the world for Christ, and Christ for the world. Mary is well
aware that human nature attributes great importance
to external signs; so she has appeared in human form on
several occasions during the past century to give men tangi-
ble proof of her lasting interest. But the question presents
itself: has Mary actually appeared in person on these occasions, and to what extent are these apparitions supernatural?

In order to get a clear notion of such phenomena, we
should consider that corporeal vision may take place in
two ways. Either a figure really presents itself to the human

eye and is seen in a natural manner; or an agent, superior to man, directly modifies the organ of vision in such a way that it produces a sensation equivalent to that which an external object would produce. The first is the usual manner. It corresponds to the invincible belief of the one who observes the apparition, and it implies a minimum of miraculous intervention, particularly if the vision is prolonged or given to several persons at once.

Here we ask: Is the figure thus reproduced to the eye the actual person it represents, or apropos of our proposition, do these apparitions of Our Blessed Lady actually bring Mary down to earth? To give an adequate answer we must consider the condition of Our Blessed Lady, such as it has been since her glorious Assumption into heaven. The soul, which is the substantial form of the body, has a natural aptitude and exigency to exist in the body to which it belongs. In consequence of which we must say that Mary is really present only where her body is, and nowhere else. There is, of course, the question of bilocation, by which the same being has been known to be in two places simultaneously. St. Thomas and other theologians deny the absolute possibility of a body to be physically present in more than one place at the time. They hold that instances of bilocation such as are found in the lives of the saints, can be explained by imaginary representations, or by aerial materialization. Other recognized theologians defend the possibility, if it is effected by omnipotent agency. If this can be true of living persons, it seems at least eminently probable that it is also possible that the bodies of our Lord and of the Blessed Virgin may become present to men without leaving the abode of glory.

But apart from actual apparitions of the Blessed Mother there is another contact which Mary makes with souls that love her Son, to the extent that she keeps very near to them. In an effort to explain this presence of the Blessed Virgin in souls we must make some general observations. Besides a so-called physical contact, there is a virtual contact, such as is characteristic of God Himself, who operates through His power. God is thus present in prime matter, in souls, and in angels, which are produced by immediate creation. It must further be noted that if God can make use of angels to produce instrumentally a properly divine effect, such as a miracle, He can also make use of the humanity of the Savior, as St. Thomas admits He does, as a physical instrumental cause to produce grace. We should then be under the direct influence of the humanity of Christ. In a similar way God can make use of Mary. But in both instances it is virtual contact, rather than physical—somewhat similar to the virtual contact of the sun which gives us light and warmth from afar.

In addition we mention with Father Garrigou-Lagrange, that God can also use a purely spiritual act as instrument, such as an interior prayer, in which case the power productive of grace is transmitted without a corporal medium. The human soul, in so far as it is spiritual, transcends the body, and its actions are not confined to the body. Although the soul has a natural aptitude for existing in the body, in itself it is absolutely simple. It is not wholly immersed in matter; its highest operations and aspirations go far above the organism, and are intrinsically independent of it. This explains how souls, in the measure in which they grow spiritually and become more and more detached from the senses, bring themselves nearer to God, and to one another as well. This can also explain a gradual increase of proximity of Mary, and define her ever-growing spiritual presence in the soul.

To this possible spiritual presence of Our Lady there must be added an affective presence which, as St. Thomas remarks, is a very real presence. In treating of the unitive force of this affective presence, St. Thomas explains that there are two kinds of union possible: an actual union, and an affective union. The former applies to two persons who are in the same place and see each other directly. The latter proceeds from the actual remembrance of the one who is loved, and the love of this person. In order to illustrate the mutual effect of affective union, St. Thomas distinguishes a twofold aspect. The one, where the person loved is in the person who loves; and the other, where the lover is in the beloved person. The first mode is often the one more felt, while the second prevails when love becomes more disinterested and self-forgetting, and seeks the good of the other. A striking example of such affective union in the lives of the saints is found in St. Monica and St. Augustine who, far removed from each other, were nevertheless spiritually united, and therefore affectively present.

A final word must be said about the sacramental presence of our Lord in the Holy Eucharist which, while directly concerning Christ, has nevertheless a very essential relation to Mary. First, as Mother of God, Mary prepared the flesh and blood of Christ, which are contained in the Holy Eucharist as the essential spiritual food for her children. Second, in Eucharistic Communion, through Christ's flesh and blood which is taken from herself, she enters into a substantial and organic relation with her children, whereby they become dear to her and obtain a special right to her motherly care and intercession.

An unhealthy form of mysticism, however, which puts a fantastic interpretation on Mary's relation to the Holy

Eucharist, and teaches that Mary is really present in the Holy Eucharist with Christ, or at least that a part of her flesh and blood is contained therein, has been repeatedly condemned by the Church. The theory also, which sees in the Holy Eucharist "relics of the Blessed Virgin," has been rejected by Rome as "false, dangerous, and scandalous." Instead of emphasizing a formal, or even a merely material identity of Christ's flesh and blood with that of Mary's in the Holy Eucharist, it should rather be stressed that, by her will Mary cooperated formally and directly in the preparation of the Holy Eucharist. In her capacity of Virgin Mother of God and spiritual Mother of her children, Mary thus remains thoroughly faithful to her charges, realizing as she does, that nothing will further our spiritual growth in her Son so much as will a true devotion to the body and blood of her divine Son, who alone is actually and substantially present in the Holy Eucharist.

CHAPTER 22

MIRROR OF JUSTICE

Justice is a moral virtue which inclines the will to render to one and all what belongs to each. In its highest form, as justice in regard to God, it is closely related to the virtue of religion. It is aided by the gift of piety, one of the seven gifts of the Holy Spirit, and becomes a habitual disposition of devoted love of God. The Blessed Virgin exercised this virtue in a notable manner when she consecrated herself to God irrevocably, and made her vow of perpetual virginity;

when she offered her divine Son to His heavenly Father at the presentation in the Temple; when she made her final offering of Him on Calvary and acquiesced in His mournful death on the Cross.

But justice also concerns the neighbor. Together with charity it regulates man's intercourse with his fellow men, for the moral virtues are in man's soul according to the degree of his charity. Regulated as Mary's justice is by this divine charity, and impregnated by the corresponding gift of the Holy Spirit, it exhibits all the characteristics of motherly devotion. This motherly devotion finds its foundation in the heart rather than in the mind.

Father Scheeben observes that in the mystical body of Christ the analogy of the physical organism generally holds true in a higher manner and in a fuller measure than in any other human grouping. For this reason there exists between Mary and Jesus the same mutual relation as there is between the heart and the head in the physical body. As the heart of the mystical body, Mary appears as the privileged seal of the Holy Spirit, who is the soul of the mystical body and proceeds from the Head to animate the whole. Thus Mary is shown as the member in whom the entire life of the Head is reflected in the most perfect manner, and who conditions and supports the influence of the Head on the other members. Moreover, this representation strikingly characterizes her personal position in the internal organism of the body of Christ, as contrasted with that place which belongs to Christ's official representatives in the external organism of the Church. Evidently Mary's mission did not include a participation in Christ's public activity. Her cooperation with our Lord and His mystical body was from the beginning and forever remains a silent, hidden cooperation in its inner activity, and in the interior communication of His life to the members. For that very reason she cooperates precisely in that activity by which Christ preeminently discharges His mission as Redeemer.

This particular inner character of Mary's activity is especially evident in the sacrifice of her Son on Calvary. While Christ poured out His blood and gave forth His divinely vital strength for the salvation of mankind, Mary spent the salutary activity of her compassion as a true and perfect maternal production. She was indeed well adapted to represent the Church at the foot of the Cross, more so since, by the voluntary offering of her Son, she effectively communicated to men the life of grace.

The symbolic representation of Mary as the heart of the mystical body is not universally used, although it is found implicitly in some early writers; explicitly in the works of Ernest of Prague. It is richer, deeper, and more characteristic of Mary's office in the Church than is the custom of depicting Our Lady as "the neck of the mystical body," as is sometimes done by mystical writers. The latter expression originated with St. Bernardine of Siena, and represents Mary as the connecting link which projects from the body and is lifted heavenward with the head. Pius X quotes it in one of his encyclicals, and speaks of "the neck which unites the Head to the members and transmits thus all spiritual gifts to the mystical body." This does not express the intrinsic relation of Mary with the work of the redemption as clearly as does the heart, which represents the vital organ of the body, being at once the seat of life and holiness.

Although this symbolic representation of Our Lady has

direct reference to her essential place in the mystical body, it seems proper at this moment to insert a few notes on devotion to the Immaculate Heart of Mary.

The devotion to Mary's Immaculate Heart finds its origin in the Gospel where Mary's heart is first mentioned in Simeon's prophecy, as a result of which we have the reproduction of Our Lady's heart, pierced by a sword. Another Scriptural passage mentioned by St. Luke on two occasions, reminds us that Mary kept all the sayings and doings of Jesus in her heart, that she might ponder them and live by them. The devotion grew when both the Fathers and the Liturgy began to apply the Canticle of Canticles to the loving relations between God and the Blessed Virgin, and the heart of Mary was readily identified with the Spouse of the Canticle. St. Augustine praised Mary as more blessed for having borne Jesus in her heart than for having conceived Him in her flesh; while St. Leo states that, through faith and love, she conceived her Son spiritually in her heart even before receiving Him into her womb.

Toward the end of the eleventh century, or early in the beginning of the twelfth, there are indications of a regular devotion to the heart of Mary. This is evident from the famous sermon on the Twelve Stars of St. Bernard, from which an extract has been taken by the Church and used in the second Nocturn of the feast of the Seven Dolors of the Blessed Virgin (Sept. 15). From then on saints have not been lacking who advocated this devotion in a singular way. St. Mechtilde and St. Gertrude deserve special mention as two faithful adherents and advocates of this devotion. We also find Richard of Saint-Laurent, Penitentiary of Rouen in the thirteenth century, St. Thomas Becket and Blessed Herman and, somewhat later, St. Bridget, who spoke of the devotion in her Book of Revelations. Nor were the succeeding centuries devoid of devotees. But it was reserved to St. John Eudes to propagate this devotion on a large scale. Although his efforts to secure the approval of an office and feast failed at Rome, the devotion continued to grow in intensity, until Pius VI granted the Bishop of Palermo the feast of the Most Pure Heart of Mary for some of the churches of his diocese, in 1799. In the year 1805, Pius VII granted a new concession by which the feast could be more widely observed. On July 21, 1855, the Congregation of Rites approved both Office and Mass for the universal Church, although no definite command was given at the time to make the observance obligatory. That crowning honor goes to Pius XII who, in 1942, dedicated the entire world to the Immaculate Heart of Mary and imposed the solemn celebration of the feast on the universal Church to be observed annually with a proper Office and Mass on August 22.

Thus the devotion to the most loving heart of Mary has found its own, and is placed next to the devotion of the Sacred Heart of Jesus. Just as the devotion of the Sacred Heart leads us to our Lord, so devotion to the Immaculate Heart of Mary directs our thoughts to Mary's person. In the case of Christ, the heart can be regarded only as a member of His body and thus formally represents His human nature. In the case of Mary, her heart represents her interior life, her virtues and hidden perfections, her virginal love of God, her maternal love for her divine Son, and above all her motherly and compassionate love for her sinful children here below. Nor do we leave out of this devotion Mary's physical heart as the life-center of her person, since that heart is the symbol of her physical and spiritual motherhood. Thus Mary's loving heart becomes a perfect mirror of divine justice, modified and tempered by charity, and, while it reflects her eternal position in the mystical body of her Son, it is at the same time a striking replica of the heart of the Savior who, while on earth and even today, prefers to show mercy rather than justice.

CHAPTER 23

SEAT OF WISDOM

The title, Seat of Wisdom, is full of meaning and replete with unction. Like all the other glorious epithets which we attribute to Mary, this title finds its origin and foundation in the grace of her divine maternity. As connatural to her maternal state it pictures Mary as the seat of eternal Wisdom which came down from heaven to take His abode in her virginal womb. By virtue of this grace Mary has become the bodily dwelling place of the uncreated Wisdom, and is shown as a perfect image of the Father, who carried uncreated Wisdom in His bosom and brought forth His Son within Himself before time was made.

In anticipation and preparation for this singular grace of maternity, Mary received fullness of grace from the first instant of her conception. Because of this fullness of grace the Holy Spirit of God had taken possession of her and made His abode within her in a habitual manner, in a manner similar to the indwelling of the Holy Spirit in the soul of the just, by which the Spirit of God assimilates the soul to Himself in a union of substance with substance. This made her soul the recipient not only of the divine virtues of faith, hope, charity, and the cardinal virtues, but also of the seven gifts of the Holy Spirit. This, under the influence of actual grace, completed the supernatural organism and the spiritual edifice of Mary's beautiful soul, in which the Holy Spirit dwelt as in a temple. As such, Mary received together with the other gifts of the Holy Spirit, the gift of wisdom, which enabled her to discern God and divine things in the light of God; made her see eternal values with the eyes of God, while giving her at the same time a supernatural taste in order to relish them. For wisdom is first and foremost the mystery of divine life, of which love is both the principle and the end. Wisdom embraces every created reality, with God as its principal and final cause. It is the brightness of eternal light, the unspotted mirror of God's majesty, and the image of His goodness.

In Mary the indwelling of the Holy Spirit had a very special meaning. The singular grace which had made her the Mother of God is usually attributed to the Holy Spirit, and Mary assumes, together with the other titles, the name of Bride of the Holy Spirit. Since the Holy Spirit is mentioned as the supernatural principle of the producing action by which our Lord was born from His Virgin Mother, and likewise of the unifying action by which the divine and the human nature were united hypostatically in the God-man, Jesus Christ, the relationship in Mary as the Bride of the Holy Spirit must be traced back to this double aspect. But both these actions were produced by the Holy Spirit in connection with the other two Persons of the Blessed Trinity, from whom He proceeds. Thus the name of Bridegroom of the Blessed Mother must not be understood as something innate in the Holy Spirit, but rather as an attribute, since the Holy Spirit acted as the representative of the entire Trinity in its marriage with Mary. In

fact, this title is specifically used to distinguish this marriage from a common human marriage, and to raise it
above the latter as a divine marriage. It characterizes the
marriage of Mary as a purely spiritual and completely holy
state, and the marriage act as the purest expression of holiest love. The result of this marriage is the closest indwelling of the Bridegroom in the Bride as His holy temple.
This specific relation brings special honor to Mary, as the
Mother of God, since her dignity is thus brought into the
closest union with each Person of the Blessed Trinity. It
likewise brings honor to the Holy Spirit, when He appears in no way excluded from the glory, power, and
benevolence, which the other two Persons reveal in Their
relations to Mary. On the contrary, a special relation is
attributed to the Holy Spirit which answers to His own
specific character of Sanctifier. On the other hand, this particular sanctifying action of the Holy Spirit is no mere
attribute, since it brings about in Mary, at least implicitly
and indirectly, a personal relation to the Holy Spirit, who
dwells in her in a certain sense bodily, and in a natural
way.

There is still another reason why Mary is called, and
rightfully so, the Seat of Wisdom. It is because of the
special office which she holds in the internal organization
of the Church, where she communicates the graces merited
by her Son. This privilege is likewise granted her because
of her specific grace of divine maternity. When we spoke
of the universal mediation of Mary we indicated her close
relation with the Church, as the mystical body of Christ.
The Church herself, as the Bride and living body of Christ,
obtains and distributes graces for all her children through
the organic interaction with her Bridegroom, or Head.
But there is in the Church no other individual or group of

persons whose prayer of intercession can represent that of
the whole Church in so cogent a manner as Mary, who, as
the very heart of the Church, was called to and was most
perfectly fitted for that office. In keeping with her position
in the kingdom of grace, and in relation to the influence
which her plenitude of grace has on the mystical body, her
natural and incessant cooperation with Christ and with
the children of Christ as the Mother of both, indeed makes
her, after Christ, the most valuable part of the mystical
body. Hence it is not surprising that the Church in her
Liturgy uses the texts of Sacred Scripture referring to Christ
Himself as the Wisdom Incarnate, in so far as wisdom is
represented as the mother and seat of all graces. We need
but refer to the text so repeatedly applied to Mary: "In
me is all grace of the way and of the truth, in me is all hope
of life, and of virtue. Come over to me, all ye that desire
me, and be filled with my fruits" (Ecclus. 24:25–26). There
is no reason why we should restrict the sense which the
Church so absolutely applies to these words and say that
Mary by her cooperation in the incarnation of Wisdom,
by which she prepared the way for the stream of Wisdom
to inundate the world, only indirectly cooperated in the
activity of Wisdom. The Church's application of these
texts to Mary requires that Mary be also regarded as the
figure of wisdom in her continual, universal, and personal
activity and power, which makes it necessary for men to
seek grace from her and in relation to her.

Thus Mary may be called the Seat of Wisdom in a very
special manner. Whether we consider uncreated Wisdom,
represented in Jesus Christ, or the wisdom of God, em-
bodied in the Holy Spirit, Mary shows a relationship to
divine Wisdom which is totally unique and unequaled in
creation. As the permanent seal of God's own wisdom,

Mary began her sanctifying work on earth in moral union with the same Holy Spirit, and continues to control the interior life of all of God's children throughout the ages.

CHAPTER 24

CAUSE OF OUR JOY

Mary is the cause of our joy because she is our Mother and our Mediatrix, standing between us and her beloved Son. The term "cause," in its philosophic connotation, is sometimes defined as one object followed by another, where, if the first object had not been, the second would not have existed. While this description does not solve the problem of causality in its entirety, it nevertheless shows the relation of cause and effect, and indicates the producing power of the one in regard to the other. Mary is the cause of our joy since she has brought joy into the world, and, as the living expression and the instrument of God's helping mercy, she is the formal motive of our hope.

The life of a Christian is essentially a supernatural life. Christ, by His merits of redemption, made this life possible, but, next to God and in cooperation with Christ, Mary is truly the secondary principle of this redeeming grace. Some Protestants still believe in the divinity of Christ. Hence they acknowledge that the fruit of Mary's womb is truly the Son of God. But they wish to say little, or rather nothing, about Mary's exceptional dignity and activity as Mother of God in the order of grace. Still this specific activity, resulting from the grace of her divine

motherhood, and resting upon her unique relation to the
Holy Spirit and His power of sanctification, invests Mary
with such a sanctifying power of her own, that only the
direct power of the Holy Spirit overshadows it. Not without reason does the Church liturgy apply the words of
Sacred Scripture without reserve, comparing Mary to a
river of a mighty water, and an aqueduct coming out of
paradise (Ecclus. 24:41). Even from ancient times Mary
was called the treasury of grace, or the throne of grace,
because of her cooperation in the redemption. All the
graces of redemption are specifically intended for the communication, the production, the nourishing, and the completion of the life of grace.

Mary's operation in the distribution of grace shows a
close relationship to the eternal operations of the Blessed
Trinity. In the mystery of the Blessed Trinity the Holy
Spirit comes forth from both Father and Son as the necessary product of Their essential love. In an analogous manner, Mary, the Mother of the divine Word, is connected
with our Lord because the divine Word through His love
gives her His person and assumes her into a union with
His person, which, although not constituting an essential
union, is the closest imaginable in any relation between
two persons. The result is also analogous. Just as the Holy
Spirit is the specific bearer and representative of the sweetness of that divine love, so the Mother of God likewise
bears this characteristic in her own degree. Among the
many reasons why Mary distributes grace is this—that she
loves grace more than anything in the world—more than
her own life—because with grace she gives her Son to us
in a most effective manner. This, indeed, constitutes Mary
as the motive of our hope: a firm hope, which is certain
in its tendency to salvation.

Mary is also the motive of our joy, for in our devotion to Mary we discover more than a friendly interest. We find the truly maternal love for her children whom she spiritually conceived and brought forth as children of God in order to perfect them in and with her first-born Son, thereby to win and possess them also as her own. In this process she obtains for us the hidden treasure of spiritual joy, a joy which no one can take from us because it is our birthright in the spiritual kingdom of God.

Nowhere do we find a better summary of Mary's claim to the present title than in the little anthem of our Blessed Lady, the *Salve Regina*. She is, indeed, the cause of our joy because she is our life, our sweetness, and our hope, to whom we turn, full of confidence, in this valley of tears. Pope Leo XIII was so devoted to this beautiful song of praise, that he prescribed it to be said after every low Mass, in conjunction with other prayers, to secure Mary's intercession for the universal Church.

Because of its intrinsic beauty and its direct bearing on the present title, together with the general esteem which this anthem enjoys throughout the Church, we here add a few annotations about its origin. The authorship is generally ascribed to Hermann Contractus, a Monk who died in 1054. The closing words, "O Clement, O Loving, O Sweet Virgin Mary," are often ascribed to St. Bernard because of a legend which originated in the sixteenth century. In the "Life and Times of St. Bernard" mention is made of a double legend, one of them relating that when the Saint was acting as legate apostolic in Germany, he entered the Cathedral of Speyer on Christmas Eve 1146; he heard the processional chanting of the anthem and, when the last words were sung, he genuflected three times. According to the more common version, the Saint moved by a sudden inspiration added the triple invocation there for the first time. Plates of brass were laid down in the pavement of the church, to mark the footsteps of the man of God for posterity, and the places where he so touchingly implored the clemency, the mercy, and the sweetness of the Blessed Virgin Mary.

Perhaps, because of the devotion of St. Bernard to the Mother of God and his diligence to spread the use of the anthem, it was introduced in Citeaux in the middle of the twelfth century. Regulated by various decrees of general chapters, it has been used in the Order of the Cistercians as an anthem of praise to their Mother, and is sung daily, with the exception of Holy Thursday and Good Friday. Nor have the other religious orders failed to use this antiphon as an expression of their filial love. The Dominicans have sung it each day since 1221; the Carthusians also use it daily, at least, since 1239, and most probably from the very foundation of the Order by St. Bruno in 1084. The Carmelites say it after every Hour of the Office. The Franciscans incorporated it into their Breviary around the year 1250, whence it has entered into the Roman Breviary to be used at the end of Compline during a large part of the ecclesiastical year.

The anthem figured largely in the evening devotions of the confraternities and guilds which were formed in great numbers about the beginning of the thirteenth century. In France, this service was commonly known as the "Salut"; in the Low Countries as the "Lof"; in England and Germany simply as the "Salve." According to Father Thurston it seems certain that our present Benediction services have resulted from the general adoption of this evening singing of canticles before the statue of Our Lady. In the course of the sixteenth and seventeenth centuries, this evening devotion became connected with the exposition of the Blessed Sacrament, which was celebrated at first only as an adjunct to lend it additional solemnity.

On various occasions the *Salve Regina* has been attacked and has been the subject of vigorous controversy. Luther complained that the anthem was sung everywhere throughout the world, and that the great bells were rung in its honor. He particularly objected to the words, "Queen of mercy, our life, our sweetness, our hope." The Jansenists had a similar objection and wished to change the wording to have it read, "the sweetness and hope of our life." Regardless of all the objections it has survived the centuries on every one of the five continents, and is chanted whenever Catholics come together to praise their heavenly Queen. As far as our country is concerned, it forms a part of our heritage, for it has been historically established that the sailors of Columbus sang this hymn on their vessels, and were instrumental in introducing it among the early Indians.

CHAPTER 25

SPIRITUAL VESSEL

This title embraces a number of Mary's privileges which have been touched on before. For the sake of unity we summarize a few of them and group them together. In regard to the variety of graces which Our Lady received, we may make a theoretical distinction. Her first grace in the order of time, was her state of habitual or sanctifying grace. This grace raised Mary to the dignity of child of God and made her a temple of the Holy Spirit. In this sense she may be called a spiritual vessel, inasmuch as all souls in the state of sanctifying grace are spiritual vessels of God. But Mary is a chosen vessel of the Holy Spirit in a special way. For the Holy Spirit had taken possession of her, even from the first instant of her creation, with a singular fullness or plenitude, so that the Angel could greet her, "Full of Grace."

This fullness of Mary's habitual grace cannot be separated from her grace of divine maternity, since the first grace was a worthy and proportionate preparation for the latter. Preparatory to her participation in the work of the redemption, the Holy Spirit took possession of Mary in a manner unknown in any other creature. She was under His constant and direct guidance and, not meeting with any obstacle on Mary's part, He possessed her in a manner similar to, or rather, far surpassing the state of transforming union which we find in the greatest saints. In the actual birth of our Lord, the Holy Spirit was the supernatural principle of the unifying action, through which our Lord assumed human flesh for our redemption; and at the same time Mary could become the chosen spiritual vessel, or Mother of our Lord. The producing action, which is also ascribed to the Holy Spirit, made Mary the chosen tabernacle of the Most High in a manner analogous to the humanity of Christ, which was sanctified by the indwelling of the divine nature.

This double grace which made Mary the Mother of God, is in itself a substantial grace, or rather the substantial grace by pre-eminence. Essentially, it is the divine being of her Son granted to the Mother and infused in her. But it is a substantial grace also in a secondary manner, since the divine Person of her Son is connected with her in a substantial and physical way. Apart from the former, however, this makes her grace one which is principally given for the benefit of others. Mary's grace of divine motherhood is first and foremost a grace which sanctifies herself. It does so in a wholly unique manner, for it puts her in possession of uncreated Grace and sets up a relation to Christ, which enables her to obtain sanctifying grace and communicate the possession of it to others.

This concept of the divine motherhood, which is based on the analogy of the hypostatic grace of Christ, is duly reflected in the writings of the Fathers, when they explain the words of the Archangel Gabriel. "Full of Grace," they say, is Mary's proper name which expresses the distinguishing mark of her person, as the name of Christ is the distinguishing name of her Son. Mary's title of "Full of Grace" directly refers to her divine maternity, and indirectly to the hypostatic union by which the two natures of Christ were united in one Person. There is, however, an essential difference between the two graces of Jesus and Mary. While Christ is consecrated and anointed by His own operation, and is the effused oil itself because of the divinity of the eternal Word, Mary is consecrated as a creature and not by herself. In this manner Mary becomes a dwelling place of God, or a spiritual vessel, consecrated entirely to God.

These graces of both Jesus and Mary constitute the foundation of their mediation between God and man. This is evident at once in the case of our Lord. For His mediation is an ineffable union and intercourse of God with creature and of creature with God, made possible by the fact that Christ assumed a human nature. As man, He is at one with the human race. As God, He is united in the most real and intimate fashion with the Father, from whom He proceeds, and with the Holy Spirit, whom He breathes forth. In the world, and at one with the world, He reaches into the innermost recesses of the Godhead. At the same time He raises the world up to the closest proximity, the most intimate union with the eternal Father, and in the Father with the Holy Spirit. In fact, He links God and God's creature together in so close a mutual relationship that the infinite distance which nature itself sets up between creature and God, is surmounted and abolished. The immediate effect of this union is a bond of the creature with God by which the substantial unity between the Father and the Son is communicated to the creature. Thus, the inspiring words of our Lord, spoken at the Last Supper, are made eminently possible: "That they may be one, even as We are one: I in them and Thou in Me; that they may be perfected in unity" (John 17:22–23).

Mary's power of mediation is indirect, and subordinate to our Lord's. While He constitutes the direct link with the human race through His adoption of a human nature, Our Blessed Lady furnished the organic link which connects mankind with Christ. Our Lord's spiritual paternity is therefore founded upon His double capacity as Incarnate Son of God and Head of all mankind, while Mary's spiritual motherhood of men is based upon her divine maternity on the one hand, and upon her organic and substantial relation to mankind on the other.

The title we now consider emphasizes this close relation with Jesus, and names Mary the Spiritual Vessel of the Word Incarnate. When she was chosen the instrument of God to make the Incarnation a reality, she also became a chosen vessel of God's own Holy Spirit, and it remains her privilege to pour this same Holy Spirit upon us, in due proportion and in a measure commensurate to our capacity, according to the words of the prophet: "I will pour forth of My Spirit upon all flesh" (Joel 2:28).

CHAPTER 26

VESSEL OF HONOR

In this title we consider, in somewhat greater detail, Mary's particular glory implied in her selection as the organic link which joins humanity to Christ. When Mary was selected by God to share effectively in the work of our Lord's redemption, an honor was bestowed upon her which is best expressed by Our Lady's title of Second Eve. This title was universally accepted as early as the second century, and the Fathers who taught it did not regard it as a fruit of personal speculation, but as the traditional doctrine of the Church. It is supported by the words of St. Paul, who describes our Lord as the Second Adam and the Author of salvation. "As from the offense of the one man the result was unto condemnation to all men, so from the justice of the One the result is unto justification of life to all men" (Rom. 5:18). In order to establish Mary as the Second Eve, the Fathers explained St. Paul's text in direct connection with the first and fundamental promise of the Redeemer, given by God in the Protogospel: "I will put enmities between thee and the woman, and thy seed and her seed: she shall crush thy head, and thou shalt lie in wait for her heel" (Gen. 3:15). Their reasoning followed a uniform pattern. The redemption, as an antidote to the cunning of the devil, was to take a course which would answer to that of the fall. The fall of the human race was brought about by the devil with the help of a man and a woman. Hence Satan had to be defeated not by the New Adam alone, but with the cooperation of a New Eve. Both sexes had their share in effecting the fall. Both sexes are to be represented in bringing about the restoration. If this had not been God's intention, the indication of a woman in the enmities announced to the devil, would be void of meaning. In this connection, we quote Pius IX, who says: "With the words 'I will put enmities between thee and the woman, and thy seed and her seed,' God in His very first announcement to the world gave the sovereign remedy which His divine mercy had prepared for the renewal of the human race. The Fathers teach us that this divine announcement clearly and distinctly points to the merciful Redeemer of the human race in the person of the only-begotten Son of God, Jesus Christ, and designates the most Blessed Virgin Mary as His Mother. It expresses very notably the enmities of both against the devil. Wherefore Christ, the Mediator between God and man, upon assuming our human nature erases the handwriting of the decree which was against us, and fastens it as conqueror against the Cross. Likewise, bound to Him by the closest and most indissoluble bond, the most holy Virgin carries into effect, together with Him and by Him, the perpetual enmities against the poisonous serpent, and crushes it by her immaculate foot."

The words of St. Augustine are even more explicit. "It is a great sign," he says, "that, as death came to us by a woman, life was born to us by a woman, so that in both sexes, feminine and masculine, the devil might be tormented in complete defeat. He would not have been adequately punished if both had not cooperated to effect the liberation." And at another occasion: "Because man fell through the female sex, he is restored by the same sex. By a woman came death; by a woman, life." St. Jerome adds the classical expression: "Death by Eve; life by Mary."

In the attempt to give a concrete explanation of this doctrine, we may proceed in the following fashion. As the first Eve was taken from the side of Adam in unity of nature, and formed one flesh with Adam, according to the words of the Lord: "Let us make him a help like unto himself" (Gen. 3:18), in similar manner Mary was placed next to our Lord. The similarity which God intended in Adam and Eve's unity of nature, was principally a similarity of soul, which was created directly by God. In keeping with the analogy, the similarity which exists between Christ and the Second Eve must also be one of divine principle. The human nature of Christ forms hypostatically one person with the divine Word through the influence of the Holy Spirit, who Himself, as the Fathers explain, proceeds from the side of the Son. In similar manner Mary possesses in the Holy Spirit a substantial principle of holiness which proceeds from the divine Word and dwells in her through grace. Thus Mary appears next to Christ as a person similarly constituted by one and the same divine principle, which is the Holy Spirit, and is placed in a relation to Christ analogous to the relation in which Eve stood to Adam, that is, of having been formed spiritually from His side and being made a help like unto Himself by God.

The soundness of this teaching becomes still more evident when we consider Mary as the prototype of the Church. As Bride of Christ and Mother of Christians, the Church stands between Christ and His spiritual children as a supernatural and heavenly principle, arisen from the side of Christ. Animated by the Holy Spirit the Church is similar and equivalent to Christ, and forms a helper like unto Himself. This idea must be particularly insisted on, because, in its application on Our Lady, it characterizes her cooperation with Jesus Christ in the redemption as a kind of bridal cooperation, and emphasizes Mary's complete dependence, as well as her closest union with the Redeemer. At the same time it establishes the fact that both factors in the divine economy of the redemption could and had to cooperate, so that the whole work could be ascribed to each, while a perfect subordination of one to the other was maintained.

There is still another aspect in which the course of redemption answers to that of the Fall. This, as the Fathers emphasize, is founded upon Mary's free consent and brings out, in their contrast, the similarity of means used in the redemption to defeat the devil. In this connection St. Justin says: "The Son of God became man that He might undo the disobedience coming from the serpent, in the same way as it began. For Eve accepted the word of the devil and brought forth death and disobedience. But the Virgin Mary, filled with faith and joy, answered the Archangel Gabriel's tidings: 'Be it done to me according to thy word'" (Luke 1:38). To this St. Irenaeus adds: "The knot of Eve's disobedience was loosened by Mary's obedience. If Eve had disobeyed God, Mary was persuaded to obey Him, so that the Virgin Mary should become the advocate of Eve. As the human race is made subject to death by Eve, so it is saved by Mary. The scale is put at an equal balance, that is, disobedience is offset by obedience."

To bring out the full import of Mary's cooperation in the redemption, especially against Eve's wrongdoing, the preceding consideration might suffice. Yet there are other reasons, apart from Eve's participation in the sin, which warranted Christ's incarnation by a human mother. (1) In the redemption, since it is the work of the triune God, both the Persons who proceed from the Father, not only the Son but also the Holy Spirit, must be represented by a special created agent. (2) Not only to a created nature, but also to a created person God wished to give the honor of cooperating in His sublime work, in order thus to make the abundance and graded regulation of the communication of His grace richer and more harmonious. (3) A human being, one to be redeemed, and hence participating passively in the redemption, was to take an active part in the execution of the redemption, in the name of the rest of mankind. (4) Finally, because of the participation of a woman (specifically destined to be associated with Christ, and who, as the maternal bride of Christ, became in her cooperation with Him the spiritual mother of the remaining members of the redeemed) the other members will have greater confidence of receiving the fruits of redemption.

CHAPTER 27

SINGULAR VESSEL OF DEVOTION

In view of her close association with Jesus in the work of redemption, it is evident that Mary was predestined from all eternity to a degree of sanctity unequalled in the history of mankind. Her measure of grace not only surpassed the measure of all human beings, but of angels as well, even the most exalted. The Church has held this in all ages, especially since the Council of Ephesus (431), for it seems consonant with God's honor that He bestow upon His Mother such holiness as would enable her to fulfill her services to Him most worthily, that she might attain to a state of sanctity like unto His. It would have been inconsistent with her sublime calling as Mother of God, through whose mediation the source of grace was given to the world, if she had not been the first to benefit by this grace. Nor would it have been fitting that she, from whom Christ willed to receive bodily life, should have no greater share than others in His divine life.

The Fathers, very appropriately, apply the words of Isaias to the Mother of Christ: "In the last days the mountain of the house of the Lord shall be prepared on the top of mountains, and it shall be exalted above the hills, and all nations shall flow unto it" (Is. 2:2). Although these words have direct reference to the Church of Christ, they have been continuously explained to refer to Mary also, as remarks St. Gregory the Great: "The Blessed Mary, Mother of God, ever a virgin, can be described by the name of this mountain. For she was the mountain that surpassed in height every chosen creature by the dignity of her election." To this Basil of Seleucia adds: "Who does not marvel at the measure in which Mary surpasses all those whom we venerate as saints? If God bestowed so much grace on His servants, what kind of virtue can we expect in His Mother? Must it not exceed the virtue of those who are subject to her? If Peter was called blessed and had the keys of the kingdom consigned to him, she before all others should be proclaimed blessed to whom it was given to bring forth Him whom Peter orally avowed. If Paul was called a vessel of election, because he carried forth into the world the name of Christ, what kind of vessel must be the Mother of God, who gave Christ to the world?"

While the preceding words establish Mary as a singular vessel of devotion because of her selection as Mother of God, they also lay the foundation of our objective devotion to Mary as Mother of Christians.

In foretelling the excellent dignity of Mary as the mountain on the top of mountains, it seems significant that the prophet says: "In the last days . . ." This we may understand in the biblical sense of St. Paul, who informs us that the final age of the world, the age of salvation, has come (I Cor. 10:11). It may also be understood in the meaning of St. Grignon de Montfort, who states that devotion to Our Blessed Lady will be more specially necessary in the last days of the world, when Satan will make an effort "to lead astray, if possible, even the elect" (Matt. 24:24). Less than four years after Pope Pius IX declared the dogma of the Immaculate Conception, Our Lady appeared at Lourdes to a young peasant girl, Bernadette, and for the greater part of a century Lourdes has been a place of miracles, a true bastion of faith against the materialistic deception of the world. When, somewhat later, communism started up as a more diabolical form of materialism, Our Lady appeared at Fatima in Portugal, warning the world against impending disaster. Pius XI observes, that much of the confusion and chaos about us is due more directly to the inactivity of Christians than to the effectiveness of the feverish efforts made by the enemies of the Church. Nothing short of a complete revision of spiritual values can save the world, and to take our cue from Mary this seems the sensible thing to do. Pope Pius XII made the first move in 1942, when he dedicated the entire world to the Immaculate Heart of Mary, and a growing movement has been apace ever since to make everyone join in an individual manner. When mankind was asked by Our Lady at Fatima to join in prayer and penance, she recommended not only the daily Rosary, but especially the greater development of the interior life, so that her Son may be expressed in each one of His members in a daily more-embracing fashion. This beautiful objective can be accomplished in no better way than by a complete consecration of one's life to Jesus through Mary.

For many years St. Grignon de Montfort had advocated this total dedication to our Lord through Mary as an essential requisite for those souls who aim at a very intimate union with God. Like the Christian virtues, the Saint indicates in his "Treatise on True Devotion to the Blessed Mother," this devotion grows in us with charity, advancing from the stage of the beginner to that of the more proficient, and continuing on to the stage of the perfect. The first degree is to pray to Mary from time to time. The second is one of more perfect sentiments of veneration, confidence, and love. In the third degree the soul gives itself fully to Our Lady by an act of consecration, in order to belong altogether to Jesus through her. This act of consecration consists in promising Mary always to have filial recourse to her, and to live in habitual dependence on her, so as to attain to more intimate union with our Blessed Lord and, through Him, with the Blessed Trinity present in our souls.

In explaining the devotion the Saint says: "I do not think that anyone can attain to great union with our Blessed Lord and to perfect fidelity to the Holy Spirit without being closely united to Our Lady and depending very much on her help. She was full of grace when she was saluted by the Archangel Gabriel; she was superabundantly filled with grace by the Holy Spirit when He overshadowed her; she so advanced in grace from day to day and from moment to moment as to arrive at an inconceivable summit of grace. On this account, the Most High has made her His unique treasurer and dispenser of His graces, so that she may ennoble, enrich, and elevate whom she wills, and make him enter the narrow gate of heaven. Jesus is everywhere and always the Son and the fruit of Mary. Mary is everywhere the true tree which bears the fruit of life and the true mother who produces it. We may apply to Mary with even more truth than St. Paul applies them to himself, the words, "My dear children, with whom I am in labor again, until Christ is formed in you" (Gal. 4:19). Mary is in labor daily with God's children till Jesus be formed in them in the fullness of His age. St. Augustine says that "the predestined in this world are hidden in the womb of Mary in order to become conformed to the image of the Son of God. There she guards, nourishes, and supports them and brings them forth to glory after death. O mystery of grace, unknown to the reprobate and little understood by the predestined!"

The devotion is a practical application of the doctrine of the universal mediation of Mary, whom divine Providence has given us as our spiritual Mother to form Christ in us. The act of consecration, as suggested by St. Grignon, reads as follows: "I choose thee this day, O Mary, in the presence of the whole court of heaven, as my Mother and Queen. I give and consecrate to thee as thy slave my body and my soul, my interior and exterior possessions, and even the value of my past, present, and future good actions, allowing thee the full right to dispose of me and of all that belongs to me, without any exception whatever, according to thy good pleasure, for the greater glory of God, in time and eternity."

In consequence of this act, the perfect servant of Mary dedicates himself to her, and through her to Jesus, that she may own his body with all its senses, keeping only the use thereof, and pledging himself to employ them in keeping with the good pleasure of the Blessed Mother and her Son. He gives her his soul with all its faculties, dedicating them under Mary's guidance to the service of God and the good of others; renouncing at the same time whatever may compromise his sanctification or imperil his salvation. He hands over to her all his interior and spiritual treasures, his merits, the value of his satisfying acts as well as the impetratory power his good actions may possess. This includes all that is communicable to others, such as prayers, good works, indulgences gained—in a word, all the merits which one can gain because of the rights of friendship with God by grace. It excludes the merits which are incommunicable, such as are gained by right of justice. These merits concern our own individual increase of sanctifying grace, with its corresponding degree of happiness in heaven. These are given to Mary that she may keep them in trust and give them their proper increase.

This act of consecration has much in common with the heroic act, by which we give to God all the satisfactory value of our actions and the indulgences we may gain, to be applied to the souls in purgatory. The act of consecration, however, is much more comprehensive, and includes all that may be given away here in life and hereafter.

The objection has been raised that making this act of consecration is like stripping oneself entirely before God of all chance to pay one's own debt, and thus one's own term in purgatory is lengthened. This was in fact the difficulty suggested by the devil to St. Bridget of Sweden, when she thought of making a similar oblation to Mary. At that occasion our Lord explained to her that the objection sprang from self-love and made no allowance for Mary's goodness and consideration. Our Lady will never be outdone in generosity, and her help to us will far exceed whatever we are able to give her.

Others wonder if making the act of consecration leaves them free to pray for close relatives and friends who may be in urgent need of our prayers. The answer is that Mary knows our obligations of charity better than we do; she would be the first one to remind us of them. On the other hand, we may be ignorant of the needs of friends and relatives, either on earth or in purgatory, and neglect to help them. Mary will be in a position to apply our good works and prayers to them, even if we are ignorant of their needs, once we have placed our spiritual services at her disposal.

Finally, the expression "holy slavery," as used by the Saint, has sometimes been criticized. This is to forget that it is a slavery of love. Bishop Garnier remarks: "If there are in the world slaves of human respect, of ambition, of money, and of shameful passions, there are also, thank God, slaves of conscience and of duty. The holy slavery belongs to this group. The expression Holy Slavery is thus a striking metaphor, opposed to the slavery of sin."

The fruits of this devotion are beyond computation. The Saint sums them up, when he says that it makes us a perfect replica of our Lord, who willed to be subject to His Blessed Mother. It is an easy, short, perfect, and safe way by which to reach Jesus. It confers great interior freedom, scruples are banished, and the heart dilates with confidence and love. It procures the good of neighbor, and especially the souls that are entrusted to our care will gain by our gift.

Living in such close proximity to Mary gives our life a unity of purpose which it could not reach otherwise. It is a perfect way of honoring our Lord, and a sure means of persevering in grace. Says the Saint: "Do not put the gold of your charity, the silver of your purity, the living waters of heavenly graces in broken vessels such as you are. Rather put all your treasures in the Heart of Mary, who is a spiritual vessel, a vessel of honor, a singular vessel of devotion."

CHAPTER 28

MYSTICAL ROSE

In the garden of God's saints there is no one who equals the Mother of God in beauty and glory. She appears next to Jesus, who Himself was spoken of by the prophet as the flower risen up out of the root of Jesse (Is. 11:1), upon whom rested the fullness of God's Holy Spirit. The Church does not hesitate to apply to Mary the symbols of the eternal Wisdom, and exalts her as the cedar of Libanus, as a cypress tree on Mount Sion, as a palm tree in Cades, and as a rose plant in Jericho (Ecclus. 24:17–18).

For ages past the rose has been considered a symbol of mystical love. Our Lady, as the chosen flower of mankind, turned toward God to receive within herself the dew of heaven, and became the throne of Emmanuel. As the sacred instrument of God in the contracting of the mystical marriage between humanity and the divine Word, Mary has given us the love of the Father through the mysterious operations of the Holy Spirit and, in the process, became the Mother of God and the spiritual Mother of men. This mystical motherhood of Our Lady is in nature real, organic, and living, and rests upon her maternal relation to our Lord, and upon the organic relation in which Christians stand to Christ. Ultimately it finds its foundation in the dignity of Mary as Bride of God and the fruitful receptacle of the divine life of grace. For, in the conception of Christ Mary received the true and eternal Word as a divine seed in such a way that, in Christ and with Him, men also must be born from it as children. Of this St. Grignon de Montfort spoke, when he said that the Holy Spirit became fruitful on earth through Mary. It was with her and of her, that He produced His masterpiece, God-made-man, and He produces daily until the end of time the predestined members of the body of Jesus Christ.

Apropos of the act of consecration to Jesus through Mary, spoken of in the preceding chapter, there exists a real mystical union with Mary. This is in addition to her moral, spiritual, and affective presence, and may be considered an effect thereof. It is the air which the soul breathes unceasingly, the atmosphere of grace, which is of vital influence in the growth of the soul. By this mystical presence of Our Lady her motherhood reaches its completion, and the Incarnation of Christ is prolonged until the end of time, even carried over into eternity.

Some souls are favored with this special grace, as was Father Chaminade, who mentions it from personal experience. "There is a gift of the habitual presence of Mary—very rare indeed, but obtainable through great fidelity." Father Neubert, who explains these words, says that they refer to a normal and habitual mystical union with Mary. A venerable servant of God describes it in this manner: "I do not see her, but I feel her presence as the horse feels the hand on the rein." Another servant of God, Marie de Sainte-Thérèse, has words to the same effect. "That sweet Mother of mine," she says, "has taken me under her maternal direction, just as a teacher takes in her own the hand of the child she is teaching to write. She remains almost uninterruptedly before my soul, drawing me to herself in so loving and motherly a fashion, stimulating me, guiding me, instructing me in the way of the spirit and in the perfect practice of the virtues. I do not lose for a single instant the charm of her presence along with that of God." Some souls, however, who have experienced great intimacy with Our Lady, say that they never experienced her actual presence within, but rather her presence very near them.

Like all spiritual growth this intimacy of the soul with Our Lady is a gradual process, and a natural result of a complete consecration to Jesus through Mary. Our Blessed Mother loves to express in the soul who trusts her, her own image, and this she does in order to transform the soul to the image of her Son. Before all else she will make this soul an imitator of her own blessed humility, as says St. Grignon de Montfort: "The humble Mary will make you a sharer in her deep humility, so that you will despise yourself and no one else, and you will love to be despised.

"She will give you a share in her faith also, which was greater than the faith of the patriarchs, the prophets, the apostles, and of all the saints. She herself has that faith no longer, for she sees all things clearly in God by the light of glory, but she keeps it in trust of her most faithful servants.

"The more you win her love, the more you will have purity of faith, which will make you set little store by the sense-perceptible and the extraordinary; a faith living and animated by charity which will make you act from a motive of pure love; a faith firm and immovable as a rock, which will make you stand strong in the midst of storms and afflictions; a faith active and penetrating which, like a mysterious master-key, will give you entry to all the mysteries of Jesus, and into the heart of God Himself; a courageous faith which

will make you undertake and accomplish great things for
God and for the salvation of souls; a faith that will be your
flaming torch, your divine life, your hidden treasure of divine wisdom, the all-powerful weapon, yours to use for the
enlightenment of those who are in darkness and the shadow
of death, to inflame those who are lukewarm and who need
the purified gold of charity, to restore to life those that are
dead by sin, and to resist the devil and all the enemies of
salvation."

Sustained by this devotion, our hope and trust in God will
soar to new heights because of our firm confidence in Mary
and her guidance. The strength of this confidence is explained by the manner of approach, for, "henceforth," the
Saint says, "we approach Jesus no longer alone, but in the
company of His Mother."

Most of all we shall grow in divine charity, under the influence of her who is called the Mother of fair love. Our
Lady will take out of our heart every scruple and servile
fear. We shall run in the commandments of her Son with
the holy freedom of the children of God. Ours will be a
childlike converse with God, whom we look upon as our
own good Father and whom we seek to please at all times. If
we have the misfortune to offend Him, we shall at once ask
humble forgiveness, stretch out our hand to Him again, and
continue on our journey to God with trust unshaken.

There is one more advantage in following Mary so closely.
We shall be one with her in mind and spirit to the extent
that her intentions become ours, while our own are lost in
those of Mary. Thus we enter into the mystic ways of Mary,
and dressed with her virtues, adorned with her grace, we
shall fly into the arms of God, where formerly our ascent
was painstaking and at best very slow. In Mary all things are
relative to God, for she is like the echo, always reflecting

Him. We can never think of Our Lady but she thinks of God for us. Thus we advance into a new era, that of reaching God through Mary in the manner of mother and child, akin to our Lord, who first chose Our Lady to be His own Mother.

CHAPTER 29

TOWER OF DAVID

Tower of David is a title of Our Lady which has its foundation in the Old Testament. The original tower of that name was the tower of the citadel on Mount Sion, which King David took during his campaign with Jebus, King of Sion. When he became king over the United Tribes of Israel, David contemplated making Jerusalem the political and religious center of God's people. He therefore assembled all the forces of the nation at Hebron, and advanced against the Jebusites, who were securely entrenched on Mount Sion. Following a long and difficult siege, David took the castle, expelled the Jebusites and lived there with his people, calling the stronghold "The City of David" (II Kings 5:9). Since towers are symbols of strength and beauty, the tower of the citadel became known as "Tower of David," reflecting, as it did, the power and integrity of the Ruler of Israel. As such, it is also a fitting symbol of Mary, who is the tower of strength and beauty in the City of God.

The title also includes a personal reference to King David, who was a type of our Lord. David, who was a king according to God's own heart, prefigured the theocratic kingdom of the Messiah, who was predicted as the one who would sit upon the throne of David to establish his kingdom and to strengthen it with judgment and with justice; to whose kingdom there would be no end (Is. 9:7). There are other respects in which David prefigured Jesus. His name, which means "The Beloved," is attributed to the Savior; and the various incidents of David's life are considered by the Fathers as foreshadowing the life of the Savior so completely that it is difficult to find another personage in the Old Testament who resembles our Lord so much, and in so many details. Bethlehem is the birthplace of both. The shepherd life of David points to our Lord as the Good Shepherd, who gave His life for His sheep (John 10:15). David, defeating Goliath single-handed, represents our Lord who slew Satan by His death on the Cross. The Fathers go so far as to find a reference in the five smooth stones which David took to slay Goliath (I Kings 17:40), to the five wounds of Christ. The betrayal of David by his trusted counsellor, Achitophel, prefigures the betrayal of Jesus by Judas. Even David's passage over the brook Cedron reminds us of our Savior's last journey with His apostles, when He went forth with them beyond the torrent of Cedron into the Garden of Gethsemane (John 18:1).

In this connection we remark that David is more than a type of the Messiah. He is a prophet, and his Messianic psalms, the literal character of which is repeatedly indicated in the New Testament, establish him as the outstanding prophet of our Lord's suffering, persecution, and triumphant deliverance. Psalm 21, the opening words of which came to Christ's lips when He was hanging on the Cross, is an eloquent example of the accuracy of David's prophetic vision. One needs but review a few verses of this psalm to recognize in minute details our Lord's passion, which David described centuries before they became a gruesome reality. "My strength is dried up like a potsherd, and my tongue has cleaved to my mouth: and Thou hast brought me down into the dust of death. They have dug my hands and feet. They have numbed all my bones. And they have looked and stared upon me. They parted my garments amongst them; and upon my vesture they cast lots" (Ps. 21:16–19).

King David is even more than a type, more than a prophet of the Savior; he is also a forebear of the Messiah. When we look at the genealogy of Jesus we find that He is called the Son of David (Matt. 1:1). But this genealogy, as given by the Evangelist, is in reality the genealogy of Joseph, the husband of Mary, as says St. Matthew: "And Jacob begot Joseph, the husband of Mary, and of her was born Jesus who is called Christ" (Matt. 1:16). St. Augustine remarks that the genealogy was extended to Joseph as a mark of honor to the husband of Mary. Since the same Evangelist claims that Joseph was the husband of Mary, and that Christ is born from the seed of David, we must conclude that Mary likewise belonged to the house of David. This is confirmed by Jewish Law, which states that all women must take husbands of the same tribe (Num. 36:8). All this shows that the genealogy of Christ extends through Mary to His illustrious forebear, and that Jesus maintains relation with King David through His virginal Mother only. The ancestral descent thus has the explicit character of a maternal relation, since the paternal element in the procreation of our Savior was supplied by God Himself, as says St. Thomas: "The body of Christ has relation to Adam and the other ancestors by means of the body of His Mother only."

On the other hand, through the supernatural conception of Jesus in Mary, He is related to His ancestors in a much higher sense than children brought forth in a natural manner. Father Scheeben remarks that He is their son, conceived through their longing and their faith in the divine promises. Because of this explicit maternal relation which united David with the Messiah, David could not be called the father of God, in the sense in which Our Lady is the Mother of God. For, Christ is brought into relation with His forefathers to the extent only that the substance of His body is taken from them; while Mary brought forth not only the substance of our Lord's body, as the natural fruit of her womb, but the divine Word Incarnate as a person. As a result of this supernatural conception—and in this we find the specific beauty of the present title—the human sonship of Christ is extended to the whole of humanity, which would not have been the case had the conception been purely natural. A natural conception, which includes a continuation of the paternal influence, makes all men descendants of Adam, and puts them in the mutual relationship of brothers and sisters according to the flesh. But in Christ we have received the promise of the Spirit, according to the words of the prophet: "Behold a virgin shall conceive, and bear a son, and his name shall be called Emmanuel" (Is. 7:14).

CHAPTER 30

TOWER OF IVORY

There is a continuity of ideas between this title and the preceding one. Solomon's Canticle, which describes the happy relations of Christ with the Church as His Bride, contains both titles. Setting forth the graces of His Spouse in a poetic fashion, our Lord says: "Thy neck is as the Tower of David" (Cant. 4:4). A few pages further, He repeats: "Thy neck is as a Tower of Ivory" (Cant. 7:4). Since, in second application, the Church understands the entire Canticle to be the most comely expression of love and admiration on the part of our Lord for His Immaculate and ever Blessed Virgin Mother, we can understand that she does not hesitate to make these expressions her own in Mary's Litany. This title thus reiterates Our Lady's beauty and strength with greater vividness, since ivory indicates the value and durability of her power which can resist the ravages of time, and endure even into eternity.

Mary's display of power and fortitude is captivating in that it lifts us high above our human weakness. It was the strength which Our Lady avowed more than ever when she stood beneath the Cross and, with great submission of mind and will, sacrificed her Son for the salvation of the world. Among the ancient Fathers St. Ambrose refers repeatedly to the fortitude of Mary, standing at the foot of the Cross, and writes: "Whereas the apostles fled, Mary stood beneath the Cross and viewed with loving eyes the wounds of her Son, because she was looking forward to the salvation of the world." St. Rupert brings out an even more striking idea, when he pictures Our Lady's compassion as similar to the pains of childbirth in which she, with Christ, gave birth to the children of grace. Like so many other Fathers St. Albert the Great finds in her compassion a privilege which is proper only to her, and which he calls "the communication of Christ's passion." Albert goes on to demonstrate that by reason of her compassion the world is bound to a sense of gratitude toward Our Lady, which in a measure should be similar to the sense of gratitude which we owe Christ for

His sufferings. This compassion was most effective, since it included a real companionship in suffering inasmuch as Mary, by her free consent, cooperated in our Lord's passion as only a mother can cooperate, with heartfelt gratitude for the privilege of thus being able to share in the merits of Christ's sacrifice for our sanctification and salvation. St. Antoninus says: "The Blessed Virgin consummated her martyrdom by sacrificing the life of her Son, a life which she loved far more than her own, and which caused her to endure a torment which exceeded all other torments ever endured by any mortal on earth."

In view of these considerations, it is almost impossible to maintain that Mary showed any sign of physical weakness or impotence from excess of grief, when standing beneath the Cross. Some artists picture her needing the support of St. John, or of Mary Magdalene in order to prevent a swoon or fainting spell as she witnessed her Son's agony. This notion probably originated in the fact that the feast of the Seven Dolors of Mary was sometimes called the "Feast of the Spasm"—which is further emphasized by the existence of a church in Jerusalem which bears the name, "The Church of Our Lady of the Spasm." Cardinal Cajetan wrote a special work to refute the possibility of a swoon, since it would be inconsistent with Mary's fullness of grace. Her sorrows were undoubtedly so great that they could have caused her death, to say nothing of physical collapse. That our Blessed Lord Himself fell repeatedly beneath the burden of the Cross, could well serve as an analogy. The prophet says: "To what shall I compare thee, or to what shall I liken thee, O daughter of Jerusalem? For great as the sea is thy destruction" (Lam. 2:13). On the other hand we must consider that the gift of fortitude which was Mary's in a superlative degree, implies a direct action of the Holy Spirit, who takes

hold of the soul in order to give it a singular dominion over
its lower faculties. From a priori evidence it could indeed
be admitted that Our Lady needed the support of others to
keep from falling, since there would be nothing uncommon
in this. It could be considered a demonstration of kindness
and compassion on the part of those who supported her.
But it is made all very improbable by the significant "Stabat" of St. John, who wrote in his Gospel: "Now there were
standing by the Cross of Jesus His Mother and His Mother's
sister, Mary of Cleophas, and Mary Magdalene" (John
19:25). The beautiful medieval sequence *Stabat Mater,*
which the Church appropriates in her Liturgy for the feast
of the Seven Dolors of the Blessed Mother, carries out the
same idea, without any possible suggestion of weakness in
Mary, regardless of the excess of sorrow which flooded her
heart. Father LeBuffe says: "In all that turmoil, Mary stood.
In all that confusion, Mary stood. By the uprighted bed of
her dying Son, she stood. And what pen will ever describe
the first *Tre-Ore* thoughts of Mary as she kept her death
watch!" Since we can admit no sign of physical weakness in
Mary while standing beneath the Cross, we must conclude
that this particular privilege was granted her because of her
special mission to complete, although only in a subordinate
way, the sacrifice of her Son.

To complete the picture of Mary as the valiant woman,
Holy Church in her liturgy compares her with Judith and
Esther, who are both prototypes of Our Lady, one supplementing the other. Judith exposed herself to mortal danger
when she beheaded Holofernes, the archenemy of the
people. In similar manner Mary was predicted as the one
who would crush the head of the serpent and end Satan's
dominion. This she actually did, with complete disregard
of her own comfort. Esther appears in a different light as a

prototype of *Omnipotentia Supplex,* the Praying Omnipotence, when she besought Assuerus to spare her people and
to make its enemy powerless. The Church uses a reference
to Judith in the Epistle of the Feast of the Seven Dolors:
"The Lord has blessed thee by His power, because by thee
He has brought our enemies to nought. . . . Blessed art
thou, O daughter, by the Lord the most high God, above
all women upon the earth. Because He has so magnified thy
name this day, that thy praise shall not depart out of the
mouth of men, who shall be mindful of the power of the
Lord forever, for thou has not spared thy life, by reason of
the distress and tribulation of thy people, but hast prevented
our ruin in the presence of our God" (Judith 13:22–25).
"Thou hast not spared thy life" characterizes the anguish
of the Mother's soul in the sacrifice of her Son, as writes Ar-
nold of Chartres: "Whoever had been on Mount Calvary, to
witness the great sacrifice of the Immaculate Lamb, would
have beheld two altars, the one in the body of Jesus, the
other in the heart of Mary. For on that Mount, when the
Son sacrificed His body by death, Mary sacrificed her soul
by compassion." In commenting on the words of the
prophet, "I have trodden the winepress alone, and of the
Gentiles there is not a man with Me" (Is. 63:3), Richard of
Saint Laurence completes the thought, when he says: "It is
true, O Lord, that in the work of human redemption Thou
didst suffer alone, and that there was not a man who sufficiently pitied Thee; but there was a woman with Thee, and
she was Thine own Mother: she suffered in her heart all that
Thou didst suffer in Thy body."

Who has not felt the reflex of this power of Mary when all
human assistance failed, and when even the common dis-
pensations of grace seemed insufficient to carry one across
the shoals of spiritual disaster. Many a sinner who saw his

spiritual life shattered and faced total moral collapse, will acknowledge that his final power to conquer sin or break an evil habit came from the powerful help of Mary, who never failed to show her encouragement when his strength was at its lowest ebb.

CHAPTER 31

HOUSE OF GOLD

Following the analogy of the two preceding titles, this one also must be read in the light of the Old Testament. It contains a direct reference to the Temple of Solomon, which was called "the House of Gold," because of the lavish use of this metal in its construction. In this respect St. Thomas remarks: "As all in the Temple was covered with gold, so was everything in the beautiful soul of Our Lady filled with sanctity."

The soul is often called the temple of God and the dwelling place of the Most High, as says St. Paul: "Do you not know that you are the temple of God, and that the Spirit of God dwells in you" (I Cor. 3:16). If this is true of every Christian, it is even more true of Mary, the Blessed Mother of God. Her state of sanctity, by the working of the Holy Spirit, far exceeded the sanctity of every other creature. For this reason St. Albert the Great calls Our Lady the golden temple of charity, because divine charity makes others children of God, but in Mary charity was born substantially, and given to the world.

It is generally accepted that the Holy Spirit intended this

typical sense of Holy Scripture in the process of inspiration really and actually, though not immediately. Thus the material and lifeless dwelling of God on Mount Moria becomes a clear type of the spiritual and living temple of God, which is Mary. All that is mentioned in Sacred Scripture about the glory and holiness of Solomon's Temple applies to Mary intrinsically and in the highest manner. Thus, when God appeared to Solomon at night, after he had finished the House of the Lord, and said: "I have heard thy prayer and I have chosen this place to Myself. . . . My eyes shall be open, and My ears attentive to the prayer of him that shall pray in this place" (II Par. 7:11; 15), His words conveyed the secondary meaning that He had selected Our Lady as the eminent Temple of God, with the added implication that all those who pray in her shall have God's immediate and undivided attention.

St. Alphonsus penetrates the mystery even deeper. He declares that Mary was the House of Gold which eternal Wisdom chose for His dwelling on earth, according to the words of the prophet: "Wisdom has built herself a house" (Prov. 9:1). Combining the accommodated sense of Holy Scripture with the typical sense, the Saint applies the texts from the Sapiential Books, which in reality describe the origin, glory, and activity of the eternal Wisdom, exemplified in our Lord, on her who is called the "Seat of Wisdom." This is an ancient and general practice of the Church, and contains formal testimony that the Church considers Mary a true image of divine Wisdom as it appears in Jesus Christ. When divine Wisdom is represented as a person who came forth from God, who stands in actual relation to the world in which He lives and works apart from God and next to Him, taking, so to speak, a central position between God and man, we readily understand that the direct application to our Lord, and the indirect application to Mary, the Mother of God, is not only possible, but becomes inevitable.

The Mother is related to her Son by true bonds of consanguinity, and maintains, by and in her Son, corresponding spiritual relations of affinity with all the Members of the Blessed Trinity. This results in a threefold relationship which Mary has with divine Wisdom.

Our Lady's relation with the Father, who possessed the Son in the beginning of His ways, before He made anything from the beginning (Prov. 8:22), is best expressed as the relation of a favored child, a daughter, through whom the Father brought forth in time the same eternal Wisdom whom He had begotten within Himself from eternity in the distinction of persons. In this Mary also resembles the Father, since she is the only productive human principle of the human nature of Christ, just as the Father is the sole productive principle in respect to the divine nature. A correlated resemblance appears from the fact that she produced Christ in the flesh through a spiritual power, without violation of her virginity, in the manner in which the Father produced Him according to the spirit.

Mary's special relationship with the divine Word is even more evident. This relationship is directed to the Person of the Son, who, as God-man, possesses the position and the power of a divine person. For which reason He lets her participate in His own sublimity in a manner to which no other creature could attain: He makes and accepts her as His Mother, and gives Himself to her as her Son.

Mary's unique relationship with the Holy Spirit, as indicated before, has its origin in the twofold principle by which the Third Person of the Blessed Trinity is indicated as the author of the productive action which brought forth the humanity of Christ in cooperation with Mary, and who, as the essential love of Father and Son, united the two natures of the God-man, Jesus Christ, into one, for the redemption and final glorification of the creature, through union with our Lord. By virtue of this double action of the Holy Spirit in and through Mary, the divinely selected human instrument, she receives her inalienable right to the double title of Bride of the Holy Spirit, and Temple of the same Holy Spirit par excellence. St. Thomas formulates it in the following words: "Mary is called the Temple of the Lord, and the sacred resting-place of the Holy Spirit, since, by the operation of the Holy Spirit, she became the Mother of the Incarnate Word." St. Anselm, putting the same truth in a slightly different way, says: "The divine Spirit, the substantial love of the Father and Son, came corporally into Mary, and, enriching her with graces above all creatures, reposed in her and made her His Spouse, the Queen of heaven and earth."

In this sense, Our Lady is the Golden Temple of the Blessed Trinity, or the House of Gold, placed among men as a symbol of God's bounty. For in her the divine Word became incarnate and dwelt among us as an effusion of the eternal light and the source of eternal life, and a revelation of the eternal wisdom of God through the maternal activity of Mary, the Mother of God. Mary is the mirror that reflects this invading light, and, after bringing it into the world, it remains her eternal task to bring us to the full perception of this revealing light. The Lord says: "I have chosen, and have sanctified this place, that My name may be there forever, and My eyes and My heart may remain there perpetually" (II Par. 7:16).

CHAPTER 32

ARK OF THE COVENANT

The three preceding titles, as well as this one, have a close relationship, in the sense that they mutually explain and complement one another. Evidently, they all refer to Mary's divine motherhood, and represent her as the unequaled sanctuary of the Most High, under different aspects.

From time immemorial the Fathers have taught that the Ark of the Covenant, as the throne of God and the dwelling place of the Lord among His people, was a prototype of both the humanity of Christ and of Our Blessed Lady.

A detailed description of the Ark is found in the second Book of Moses. It was made of setim wood in the shape of a chest, about fifty inches long, and thirty inches in width and height. The whole was overlaid with purest gold, within and without, and a golden rim or crown ran about it. At the four corners four golden rings had been cast, through which passed two bars of setim wood covered with gold to carry the Ark. It was sheltered in its entirety by a cover of like dimensions, also of purest gold; this was called the Propitiatory, upon which were placed two cherubim of beaten gold. The two angels extended over both sides of the Propitiatory, spreading their wings and covering the oracle. While they looked toward one another, their faces were turned toward the Propitiatory as in adoration.

It is worth noting that the Law which forbade the making of any carved image lest the Israelites should fall into idolatry, allowed this exception in respect to the two cherubim.

Probably it was felt that this allowance did not constitute immediate danger to the faith of the people, since the Ark was kept hidden behind the veil of the sanctuary. Originally the Ark of the Covenant was intended to contain only the Tables of the Law, which were given to Moses. Upon subsequent command a golden vessel, holding a gomor of manna (Exod. 16:34), and the rod of Aaron, which had blossomed miraculously (Num. 17:10), were also enclosed in the Ark. This is confirmed by St. Paul, who mentions these facts in his letter to the Hebrews (9:4), although we are certain that when the Ark was placed in Solomon's Temple it contained only the tables (III Kings 8:9). The holiest part of the Ark apparently was the Propitiatory, for, whenever God communicated with His people, He spoke from there. Holy Scripture says: "When Moses entered into the tabernacle of the covenant to consult the oracle, he heard the voice of one speaking to him from the propitiatory that was over the ark between the two cherubims, and from that place He spoke to him" (Num. 7:89). The whole was covered with a cloud, which symbolized the presence of God, for the purpose of the Ark was to furnish a visible sign of God's invisible presence in the midst of His beloved people.

Throughout the Old Testament we find many passages in which the power of God is symbolized by a cloud. We mention only that God preceded the people of Israel out of Egypt, going before them in a pillar of cloud by day (Ex. 13:21). Moses went up into a dark cloud where God was, to receive the Ten Commandments on Mount Sinai (Ex. 20:21); and again, he remained with God forty days and forty nights in the cloud, at which time he received detailed directions about the construction of the tabernacle and all things pertaining to public worship (Ex. 24:18). These symbolic passages reach their climax in the prediction of the Angel, spoken to Our Lady: "The Holy Spirit shall come upon thee and the power of the Most High shall overshadow thee; and therefore the Holy One to be born shall be called the Son of God" (Luke 1:35). Here the cloud was spoken of as the vivifying power which descends from above, impregnates, and invigorates, in the manner that the Spirit of God moved over the waters when the earth was void and empty, and darkness was upon the face of the deep (Gen. 1:2). The implication of a second creation is at once evident. The Spirit of God, which originally descended over the chaos as principle of light and life, thus forming the first creation, now forms again, by the power of the Most High, the second and higher creation out of the Virgin. In this way the present title makes an obvious and distinct reference to the descent of the Holy Spirit, who overshadowed the Virgin with the personal power of the Most High, just as God once descended upon the Ark of the Covenant, in order to dwell in Mary in a more potent way than He had once dwelt in the cloud above the Ark.

St. John makes mention of the Ark as he beheld it in heaven, during his prophetic vision which he had on the Island of Patmos. "And the temple of God in heaven was opened, and there was seen the Ark of the Covenant" (Apoc. 11:19). This vision points clearly to Mary, who was bodily taken up into heaven to join the glory of her Son, as was testified to by Pius XII in his Apostolic Constitution on Mary's Assumption. Of this mystery St. Theodore of Studium says: "Today the golden shrine, which God Himself made, is removed from the terrestrial tents to the heavenly Jerusalem." While the Ark of the Covenant, as mentioned in the Old Testament, has a distinct reference to both the sacred humanity of our Lord and to the virgin body of His Mother, in St. John, the text points exclusively, or at least

primarily to Our Lady. In the Apocalypse Christ's humanity is invariably represented by the Lamb which stands on
the throne of God, above the Ark of the Covenant. The passage is directly connected with the following verse, where a
woman appeared clothed with the sun, a passage which the
Church has consistently applied to the Virgin Mother
(Apoc. 12:1).

But the Ark of the Covenant in olden times was not
simply a visible sign of God's presence among His people;
it was likewise, and very distinctly, a symbol of invincible
strength and divine assistance in the face of Israel's enemies.
Thus the Lord crumbled the walls of Jericho, and delivered
the city into the hands of Josue, after the Ark had been carried about the city in solemn procession for seven successive
days (Josue 5:20). The sacred narrative seems to suggest that
the Ark was repeatedly carried about, whenever the emer-
gency required. Finally, in the first Book of Samuel we are
told that the ancients of Israel, on their own initiative,
brought the Ark of the Covenant of the Lord from Silo, to
have it in their midst when they were hard pressed by the
Philistines (I Kings 4:3). But God was not well pleased with
His people and delivered them into the hands of the Philistines; and the Ark of God was taken, while the two sons of
Heli, Ophni and Phinees, who served as guards to the Ark,
were killed. But the Ark retained its glory even in captivity.
When the Philistines took it and brought it into the Temple of Dagon, God retaliated, and the god Dagon was found
lying prostrate upon its face before the Ark (I Kings 5:4).
Subsequently, God struck the people of Azotus with various
plagues, and when the magistrates transferred the Ark from
place to place, God chastened every city where it entered,
until after seven months, the Philistines decided to return
the Ark to its rightful owners.

In its final symbolic meaning this title thus signifies Our Lady's power and invincible strength in the face of God's enemies. It is to her that we must turn, like the people of old, for God has made a New Covenant with us, His chosen people, whereby He gave Himself and His Blessed Mother as a pledge of enduring help and lasting strength against the foes of our salvation.

For the sake of rounding off our subject, we add that we have several traditions about the destiny of the Ark after the fall of Jerusalem in 587 B.C., one of which, contained in a letter which the Jews of Jerusalem sent to their brethren in Egypt, is related in Sacred Scripture. The details are derived from the prophet Jeremias, who relates that, being instructed by God, he commanded that the tabernacle and the Ark should accompany him till he came to the mountain where Moses saw the promised land, which he was not allowed to enter. There Jeremias discovered a hollow cave; here he hid the tabernacle, and the Ark, and the altar of incense, and forthwith sealed the place. When some of them that followed him came to mark the place, they could not find it (II Mach. 2:4–6). According to many commentators, this letter which contains a quotation from a lost document, cannot be considered to be divinely inspired, since as a rule direct quotations in the Bible remain what they are, and can claim only such authority as the context may warrant.

CHAPTER 33

GATE OF HEAVEN

These words express great trust and confidence on the part of Mary's children, since they emphasize her mediation and central position between God and man. St. Bonaventure declares that no one can enter heaven unless he enters by Mary as through a door; for all graces which we call our own, come from Our Lady. This doctrine, which is theologically certain, although not yet dogmatically established, cannot be treated lightly, since it suggests the thesis that Mary's intercession before the throne of God is not only useful, but necessary. This necessity, as Father Suarez remarks, is not an absolute necessity, for the mediation of Jesus Christ alone is absolutely necessary. It constitutes, however, a relative necessity, for the Church believes with St. Bernard, that God has determined that no grace shall be granted otherwise than by the hands of Mary.

The theological arguments favoring this teaching have been treated before. Here we wish to emphasize on liturgical grounds that Mary is indeed considered the dispenser of all graces, and that mankind is thus invited by the official prayer of the Church, to seek grace in her. From early centuries the Church has applied the Sapiential texts of Sacred Scripture to Our Blessed Mother on the ground that what is said of the absolute divine Wisdom may be applied directly to Jesus Christ, as the incarnate Wisdom, and indirectly to Mary, who is the Mother of our Lord. Nor is this application made in a restricted manner, in the sense that Our

Lady, by her cooperation in the incarnation of Wisdom, prepared the way for the stream of Wisdom to enter into the world. As previously mentioned the formal application of similar texts by the Church rather demands that Mary be also regarded as a figure of absolute Wisdom, next to our Lord, in her continual, universal, and personal activity and power, which makes it necessary for man to seek grace from her and in relation to her in a formal manner. That this application is made possible at all, is bound up with God's decree by which Mary was destined from all eternity to become the Mother of God, a decree which contained all the obligations and privileges which this sublime vocation implies. As Pius IX says: "From the beginning and before all ages, God selected and prepared for His only Son the Mother from whom, having taken flesh, He would be born in the fullness of time." Besides giving us a peculiar insight into the wisdom of God, it is a consoling truth to remember that Mary was in the mind of God from all eternity, and this idea was so closely interwoven with the proposed Incarnation, that both Jesus and Mary formed but one unit in God's mind, as the combined principle of redemption. Since dogma and prayer are governed by the same law, it is an accepted axiom that the faith of the Church is manifested by her prayer. For which reason it is not only safe to adopt the method of the Church, but it also furnishes us with an ecclesiastical guarantee that our application is sound, and may be followed without any danger.

Examining the standard Office of the Blessed Virgin, we find the very words of eternal Wisdom placed upon Mary's lips, thus illustrating her transcendental position in the eternal designs. "The Lord possessed me in the beginning of His ways, before He made anything from the beginning. I was set up from eternity, and of old before the earth was made. The depths were not as yet, and I was already conceived. Neither had the fountains of water as yet sprung out; the mountains with their huge bulk had not as yet been established: before the hills I was brought forth" (Prov. 8:22–25).

Continuing in the same vein, the Church invites us to approach Mary directly and with absolute confidence, since in her are the words of divine Wisdom. "I love them that love me: and they that in the morning early watch with me, shall find me. With me are riches and glory, glorious riches and justice. For my fruit is better than gold and the precious stone, and my blossoms than choice silver. I walk in the way of justice, in the midst of the paths of judgment. That I may enrich them that love me, and may fill their treasures" (Prov. 8:17–21). Again, "Blessed is the man that hears me, and that watches daily at my gates, and waits at the posts of my door. He that shall find me, shall find life, and shall have salvation from the Lord. But he that shall sin against me, shall hurt his own soul" (Prov. 8:34–36).

We do not always realize that devotion to the Blessed Mother is no matter of choice, but of moral necessity. The Church shows unlimited confidence in Our Lady, who was and is so closely united with the mercy of God. For, by divine Wisdom our spiritual formation has been placed in Mary, the prototype of divine perfection, formed after the perfection of her own Son, who distributes her gifts with as much liberality as a mother shares her advantages with her children. Applying the words of Ecclesiasticus in the Little Office, the Church makes us realize this essential participation in Mary's privileges, while she pictures her as living in God's people, her favored heritage. "In all I have sought rest, and I shall abide in the inheritance of the Lord. Then the Creator of all things commanded, and said to me: and

He that made me, rested in my tabernacle. And He said to me: Let thy dwelling be in Jacob, and thy inheritance in Israel, and take root in My elect . . . And so was I established in Sion, and in the holy city likewise I rested, and my power was in Jerusalem. And I took root in an honorable people, and in the portion of My God His inheritance, and my abode is in the full assembly of saints" (Ecclus. 24:11–16).

Our Lady is not merely proud of her inheritance and of her privilege to enliven our inner life with the wealth of her graces; she wishes us to share in them profusely and become daily more united with the prime source of Wisdom through her efficacious mediation. She wants us to enter this paradise of delights and roam about in the life of the spirit. No one understands God and the secret working of grace as does Mary, the first and full recipient of God's own fullness through the merits of her Son. Turning to the figure of a spiritual paradise, Our Lady reminds us that she herself is the very entrance to this realm of grace. "I am the mother of fair love, and of fear; and of knowledge, and of holy hope. In me is all grace of the way and of the truth, in me is all hope of life, and of virtue. Come over to me, all ye that desire me, and be filled with my fruits. For my spirit is sweet above honey and the honeycomb. My memory is unto everlasting generations. . . . They that harken to me, shall not be confounded; and they that work with me, shall not sin. They that explain me shall have life everlasting. All these things are the book of life, and the covenant of the Most High, and the knowledge of truth. I have poured out rivers. I, like a brook out of a river of a mighty water; I, like a channel of a river and like an aqueduct, came out of paradise. I said: I will water my garden of plants, and I will water abundantly the fruits of my meadow. And behold, my brook became a great river, and my river came near to a sea" (Ecclus. 24:24–43).

Who will be able to contain the flow of graces which Mary has prepared for those who trust her, and place no bounds to their trust. Who can measure the extent of the riches of the man who disdains the wisdom of the world, in exchange for the wisdom of God. God's holy designs are no longer hidden from the interior soul; they are revealed to him by Mary. It is the secret of Mother and Son: the Son who wishes to possess us in His Mother; the Mother who wishes to own us in her Son. This is the combination which unlocks the affluence of God Himself, and the key which opens to us the door of paradise.

CHAPTER 34

MORNING STAR

When reviewing the meaning of this title, we almost instinctively turn to a parallel place in Holy Scripture where the Star of the Magi is mentioned. "Now when Jesus was born in Bethlehem of Juda, in the days of King Herod, behold, there came Magi from the East to Jerusalem, saying: Where is the newly born King of the Jews? For we have seen His star in the East and have come to worship Him" (Matt. 2:1–2).

The prophet Balaam spoke of a star which was to rise out of Jacob, and of the scepter which was to spring from Israel, the father of Juda (Num. 24:17). That star was our Lord. But all the Messianic prophecies have distinct reference to the Mother of the Messiah, and we are not surprised that the Church acclaims Mary by the same name. For Our Lady also is a guiding star, one which leads us infallibly to Bethlehem, and to the feet of the Savior.

The Liturgy employs a beautiful hymn, the *Ave Maris Stella*, the origin of which is difficult to trace. It is found in a St. Gall manuscript of the ninth century, but is undoubtedly of much older origin; some even ascribe it to St. Venantius Fortunatus, who died in 609. It was in frequent use during the Middle Ages, and forms the inspiration for several other hymns. We still use it today in the Roman Breviary, and it is sung in practically every Office of the Blessed Virgin.

> Hail, thou Star of the ocean,
> Mother of God's high estate,
> And forever Virgin.
> Blissful heaven's gate!

Like little sea-worn vessels on uncharted waters, we are tossed about by the storms of life. If we are to reach a safe harbor, we must follow the star which is sent us by God and guides us from afar. St. Bernard says: "If you wish not to be lost in the storm, keep your eyes on the Star of salvation; for if Mary is with you, you will reach paradise. When the storm of temptation arises, when you are midst the reefs and shoals of tribulation, fix your gaze upon the Star of the Sea, call upon Mary. If tossed by the rising tide of pride and ambition, if lost upon the troubled waters of scandal and contention, look at the Star, invoke her name. Do the billows of anger, of avarice, of lust batter against your soul, cast your eyes upon Mary. Does the greatness of your crime fill your soul with terror, does your wretched conscience beat you down in shame and the fear of judgment paralyze your heart; when about to sink to the depths of despondency and despair, think of Mary. In perils and in sorrows and in fears think of her, call upon her name. Let her name be ever on your lips, and the thought of her ever in your heart. Follow her, that the power of her intercession may attend you; imitate her, for in her footsteps you cannot go astray; call upon her, and you cannot despair; think of her, and you cannot fail. If she holds you by the hand, how can you fall! Under her protection, there is no fear. Under her guidance, you cannot falter. Under her patronage, you are sure to reach your goal."

Particularly charming is the entreating prayer of the *Ave Maris Stella* to share in Our Lady's kindness and purity, and the trust it displays in Mary's motherly help.

> Virgin of all virgins,
> Mild and sweet of mind,
> Freed from all transgressions,
> Make us chaste and kind.

Who does not recognize in these two virtues the foundation of all perfection, the true touchstone of sanctity, the infallible treasure of every God-loving soul? Bespeaking for themselves God's necessary presence, there are no two virtues which reflect with more exactitude and sincerity the world of grace within. They are like a true image of God's own fundamental perfections, for which reason the Church has never put her official stamp of approval on the life of one of her children who was not gentle and kind. Nor has she ever raised to the glory of the altar a person who failed to be an example of the angelic virtue, either preserved intact throughout an entire lifetime, or regained by years of candid struggle and severe penance.

Mary's gentleness is an inspiration for all who fear the

struggle against themselves and their unkind nature. In her maternal love she could guide her children only by the one way, her own way of self-forgetting, self-sacrificing devotion. Those who have grown up near Mary, grew up in this supernatural atmosphere. This attitude becomes even more evincing as the years go on. It develops into a thoughtful and deep appreciation of God's mysteries which are so closely identified with Our Lady; and a heartfelt gratitude for God's graceful design which took Mary unto Himself as the Mother of our Lord and made her the inevitable medium between God and man, next to and because of Jesus, for time and eternity.

Nor is her immaculate purity less inspiring. Her name itself breathes confidence, and as soon as we think of her in time of temptation, the evil suggestion is put to flight. Her spiritual presence is like the pure air of the higher altitudes that invigorates and gives the sensation of freedom and strength, with the result that we become like mountain climbers who pity those condemned to breathe the close air of the city.

Purity is one of the eight beatitudes which opens the gate of paradise. Mary leads us to this gate and wishes us to enter, but we are detained at the entrance as by an angel with a flaming sword, unless we are pure of heart and worthy to pass the threshold; for only the pure of heart shall see God.

We do not seem to realize how much we really cherish this virtue of purity. We love a child with its sunny smile because he radiates purity in its pristine splendor; the flowers, which have not been touched by hand; the winter snow, which whirls from the sky and covers the trees with silent beauty. Man may lose this virtue, but he cannot lose his love and admiration for it, nor his longing to recover it once again. Even the Pagans of corrupt Rome used to bow their heads when passing a Vestal Virgin, who was sworn to chastity while tending the perpetual fire on the altar of her goddess. Well could the Wise Man exclaim in wistful reverence: "O how beautiful is the chaste generation with glory: for the memory thereof is immortal: because it is known both with God and men" (Wisdom 4:1).

Since kindness and purity are such lovely virtues we grow ever more desirous of them. We cannot believe that Our Lady will disappoint us in our quest of either one, for it is her special task to lead her people across this wasteland, until the day dawns, and the morning star rises in our hearts, and we meet with God Himself, who is both Purity and Love.

A touching story of Our Lady, Star of the Sea, is recorded by Father Cooney, in the magazine *Madonna*.

There is a little Gothic church in Port Lyttelton, New Zealand, well known to many seafaring folk. It is the oldest Catholic church in the Dominion, and the ground on which it stands was given by the first Catholic Prime Minister, back in 1860.

Strangers who visit the little church cannot help noticing a large and beautiful oil painting of a three-masted French barque, called the Boieldieu, which hangs on the wall near the church door. A brass tablet beneath the picture contains the words: "Reconnaisance à Marie le 10 août, 1904." (In gratitude to Mary, August 10th, 1904). The picture is a votive offering to Our Blessed Lady from the crew of the Boieldieu.

The vessel, a large and beautiful steel barque, left Sydney on June 3rd, 1904, for Falmouth, with a cargo of wheat. All went well for the first week or ten days, but soon after rough weather and heavy seas began to prevail. The ship battled bravely against the elements for some days, but the sea became so rough and the weather so bad that on June 28th the rudder was carried away in a terrific sea. The crew set to work to repair the damage and replace the rudder, but a second and third rudder were also ripped off.

Meanwhile the vessel, with the flag of distress flying, drifted down the west coast of the South Island, N.Z. Then she was carried away below Steward Island till she reached lat. 57, S. She was now far away from the usual trade routes followed by various shipping companies, with no possible chance of being picked up by a passing steamer.

With a rough sea, and bitterly cold, antarctic weather, the ship tossed about helplessly, expecting every moment to crash on the rocks of some small island. The crew of staunch Breton Catholics, with a lively faith in the providence of God and an unbounded confidence in her who is called The Star of the Sea, decided to make a novena. They proposed to come on deck each day to recite the Rosary together and to sing the *Ave Maris Stella*. They promised, in case they were saved, that they would present the church of the port where they arrived safely with a thanksgiving offering, and with the beautiful painting of the Boieldieu which they carried on board.

After two days of novena prayer, the weather began to lift a bit and the seas became calmer. Gentle, steady, and persistent south winds blew the ship northwards toward New Zealand. She came on as steadily and as surely as if she were under steam and with a rudder guiding her, until she stood about thirty miles outside the Lyttelton Heads, which, as the Captain put it, she seemed bent on entering of her own accord. Here the Kittawa, a Union Steamship vessel which had just left Lyttelton for Timaru, sighted the Boieldieu flying the flag of distress. They went to her assistance and towed her into port.

True to their solemn pledge to Our Lady, the captain, officers, and crew of the rescued vessel, presented the little church of Port Lyttelton with a beautiful set of white vestments, which are still in use today. They had a Mass of thanksgiving, and placed the oil canvas of the Boieldieu on the wall near the entrance. The older parishioners will never forget how the entire crew of Breton sailors recited the Rosary together on that occasion, and sang the lilting strains of the *Ave Maris Stella*.

CHAPTER 35

HEALTH OF THE SICK

It is not an uncommon occurrence at Lourdes, when a miracle is witnessed, that the enthusiastic crowd spontaneously intones the *Magnificat*, Our Lady's song of triumph which praises her humility that exalted her in power above the mighty.

Mary's readiness to heal the sick is a thoughtful extension of our Lord's solicitude to give sight to the blind, hearing to the deaf, and poise to the halt and lame. It illustrates Mary's deep sympathy for human misery, a sympathy which knows no limit. There are countless miraculous statues, prints, and images, which are found in every part of the world, but particularly in European countries, because our Mother has scattered her favors with a prodigality which, according to human calculations, approximates extravagance. But in Mary's mind there is no extravagance. If those places which have seen Mary's miraculous intervention, have multiplied, it is because the needs of her children have multiplied, and Our Lady wishes to be wherever help is needed.

Among these many places of devotion where Mary has worked her miracles, the sanctuary upon the rock of Massabielle remains the outstanding place of refuge. Literally thousands upon thousands of traceable cures have been officially investigated and recorded at the *Bureau des Constatations Médicales* at Lourdes. But for every instantaneous cure of an organic disorder, there have been thousands of unrecorded healings of a spiritual nature. For Mary, like her Son, is primarily concerned about souls. Catholic spirituality in France was indeed at a low ebb when Our Lady appeared to Bernadette Soubiroux in 1858. France had come a long way since its rulers had been called "Most Christian" by the Popes of their day. Pagan philosophy and anti-clerical legislation were rapidly replacing the Concordat of Napoleon under the influence of Masonic lodges, and, when Mary indicated her wish to the little seer of Massabielle to have a chapel built on the spot, she undoubtedly expressed her heart's desire to lead the "Oldest Daughter of the Church" back to her Son by means of a sincere devotion for the Mother.

Between sin and suffering there is an intrinsic, reciprocal relationship, as between cause and effect. At the bottom of all suffering, both bodily and spiritual, there is the final reason of sin, which brought about the disintegration of human nature. Sin went so far as to try to annihilate God. But the very act which was contrived to kill God, brought about its own destruction. Sin hasn't been the same since. It can never repeat itself to the extent of again crucifying the Son of God. But it can still do unspeakable harm, persecute religion, pervert man and make him hate God. Our Lord has defeated sin in principle, made it subservient to the spirit, but He did not make it unreal. Sin still continues to assert itself in the life of man, and even the possibility of drawing away from God is a cause of suffering in the best of us. The world is one vast Golgotha. Given perfect love on the part of God and freedom to rebel on the part of man, we have historical tragedy. Because of the abuse of freedom our Mother wept on the mountain of La Salette, when she appeared to two young shepherds and said: "How long I have suffered. . . . You will do well to pray, to do good; never will you be able to make recompense for the pain I have taken upon myself."

Referring to these words of the Madonna, Jacques Maritain asks the question: "Can one weep, suffer, and know pain in Paradise?" He cautions against the facile retort that these are mere forms of expression, common enough in Holy Scripture where it is said that God repents, grows angry . . . that God looking upon the sins which brought about the flood, was touched inwardly with sorrow of heart (Gen. 6:6). We must take care that we do not lessen the truth by our commentaries; that we do not change the language of God into figures of rhetoric or exaggeration. If Our Lady wept and spoke as she did, it was because in the system of signs which men are able to understand, nothing else could better express the unutterable reality of what goes on in heaven. Those expressions which imply an imperfection or real pain incompatible with beatitude, do not err by excess but rather by defect. For everything that is in creation, inasmuch as it contains being and goodness, is in God in a virtual and supereminent manner. If there is anything good in tears, anything beautiful, then that, too, purged of all pain and of all imperfection, is in the same way by essence in God, and in those who see God by participation. The tears of the Queen of heaven are still infinitely far short of letting us understand the nature of the sovereign horror God and His Mother have of sin, and their intense pity for the wretchedness of the sinner.

In addition there are the apparitions, more and more numerous since the time of St. Gertrude, in which our Savior shows Himself to favored souls, quite filled with sadness, the wound of His heart bathed in blood. Do not these tell us, like the tears of Our Lady, that one can speak of a virtual sorrow in Jesus and Mary? Virtual sorrow—which is real sorrow—all down the ages for the ingratitude of men. During His life on earth our Lord's soul always enjoyed the beatific vision. Nevertheless by a miraculous restraint of the effects of this vision, He remained subject to suffering. One of the most sublime aspects of His suffering is this union of deep sorrow and perfect peace. St. Thomas explains this enigma in our Lord's determination to suffer for humanity. There is, indeed, more joy in giving than there is in receiving. More happiness in loving than in being loved. The more precious, lasting, and immortal the gift, the more delight there is in sharing it with others. In dying, there was extreme sorrow in Christ, but also extreme happiness. For at that precise moment Christ merited eternal life for us, bringing back to us the stream of divine mercy, as He Himself said: "I came that they may have life, and have it more abundantly" (John 10:10). Now He can no longer really suffer, because the secondary effects of the beatific vision are no longer held back. Neither can His Mother. But the causes which, in themselves and by that which is in them, bring about suffering, have not ceased to be. Is not each lost soul a fragment torn from the flesh of our Lord? Are not all of us, leprous as we are, children of our Immaculate Mother? Even if the vision of God and the state of beatitude do prevent Jesus and Mary from suffering in the accepted sense, they have sufficient cause from the conduct of men for suffering an ocean of pain.

Finally, we must not forget that when they could suffer in a human way, Mary in her compassion really wept for each one of us, and for each one of our sins, as Jesus in His passion bled for each one of us, and for each one of our sins.

It seems worthy of note that Our Blessed Lady, when she appeared at Guadalupe to a poor Indian peasant, wore as her only ornament a plain black cross enclosed in a gold circlet. This was to signify Our Lady's connection with the pains of her Son. In this respect Father Florencia, an early historian of the miraculous image of Guadalupe, writes: "Since the holy picture appeared to prepare and help with the redemption of these nations, the Mother of God, in order to move and attach them to the devotion of the Holy Cross, chose to deck and adorn herself with it, so that the Indians, seeing the esteem in which this Sovereign Lady held the Cross, might love it in like manner."

Our Lady's apparitions have always had the primary purpose of leading humanity to her divine Son. Men must refrain from sin. They must pray and must do penance for the manifold transgressions of the world. Such was the message of La Salette, of Lourdes, and of Fatima. "Men must no longer offend our divine Lord, who is already offended too much." In this glorious manner Mary provides true health for suffering humanity, and, ever true to her God-given calling, she heals souls, even before she heals bodily ailments.

CHAPTER 36

REFUGE OF SINNERS

Among creatures no one is greater than Mary. Yet, no one is more approachable, more gentle, more helpful. She is particularly kind to sinners for, with temptations as manifold as they are, and the world as enticing as it is dangerous, sinners need kindness above anything in the world. It is so easy to draw away from God. But the return road is steep and hard to travel, because sin instilled in the sinner a feeling of independence; it made him self-sufficient, sometimes brazen. Priests who have grown old in the service of God and of souls, will attest that there is no foolproof formula to deal with sinners successfully, other than the method of our Lord, which was one of kind understanding and of a loving will to be patient. "Has no one condemned thee? . . . Neither will I condemn thee. Go thy way, and from now on sin no more" (John 8:10).

Mary is the refuge of sinners precisely because she knows the irreparable damage which sin does to the soul. The sinful act which, in the eyes of God, made crucifixion a necessity, can never be fully understood by mortal man. But Mary's understanding is very close to God's own understanding. She knows that the human mind is similar to an ocean. Both have a titanic capacity for good and evil. In both there are surface undulations which hide the larger and most awe-inspiring waves that move on their mysterious courses far down in hidden depths. The disparity between saint and sinner is often far less than we believe. Both have turbulent natures with deep and ardent passions: one endeavors to reach his own selfish ends, the other submits them to the order of grace. One moment of grace can change a sinner into a saint, as it changed Saul into Paul, and turned Dismas into the glorious thief who stole paradise. In our instance it is the continual flow of grace which keeps us always moving toward God. Sudden conversions are exceptions. The usual progress in spiritual life is a rhythmic movement that is regulated by love, rather than by sudden and violent impulse.

But these unintermitting graces are not less energetic, even though less brilliant, than the lightning bolt that struck Saul on his way to Damascus. All our graces are fitted to the moment; even Paul was refused a second miracle of grace, when a messenger of Satan buffeted him and he thrice besought the Lord that it might leave him. God's answer, on that occasion, was as disconcerting to him as it is to us; "My grace is sufficient for thee, for strength is made perfect in weakness" (II Cor. 12:9). It is at such moments particularly that we can understand the maternal power of Mary's intervention. We like to think that God's sufficient graces are not seldom made superabundant through Our Lady's intercession. Here again the tears which Mary wept on the mountain of La Salette are relevant. Mary averred that she could not go on any longer; that she was forced to let fall the hand of her Son. "It is so strong and so heavy that I cannot hold it back any longer." But she *did* hold it back, and in holding it back today, when the sins of the world seem to have reached the saturation point, she shows herself more than ever the refuge of sinners.

As the spiritual mother of all, Mary has unbounded care for her poor exiled children. Bereaved of grace, we shall desire the forbidden fruit, and shall wander far into the desert to find it. The fruit, sought for by man, has beauty only to the senses, like the apples of Sodom which turn to ashes the moment they are plucked. Our Lady wants us to reach for the Blessed Fruit of her womb, which abounds in eternal beauty of both body and soul, and communicates this beauty to all who partake of Him in the union of faith and charity and full surrender to grace.

It was Mary's specific privilege to be conceived without sin, and to have avoided every sin, however slight, during the long course of her life. She alone among all humans received fullness of grace, which so filled her soul with eternal beauty that it overflowed upon her body and made her a worthy dwelling place for the incarnate Word of God. For this reason both the Archangel and Elizabeth praised her: "Blessed art thou among women, and blessed is the fruit of thy womb" (Luke 1:42). The Church continues this song of praise in the Hail Mary. For many centuries the Hail Mary was restricted to this panegyric encomium, whence it derives the name "Angelical Salutation." But the Church felt the increasing urgency of adding a petition. Taking up where the Archangel and Elizabeth left off, the Church added the last part, which transforms the Hail Mary into a prayer.

We like to ascribe the power behind this prayer to the mystery of the divine maternity. So does the Church. For, if Our Lady is the Mother of God, what doubt can we have that her power of intercession before the throne of God borders on divine omnipotence itself; not an omnipotence of justice, but one of grace. However, the main emphasis must go to our condition as sinners. This is no mere formality, not just a humble confession of our miseries in order to excite Mary's compassion, but a true avowal of our dependence on her because of our sinful condition. If there had been no sinners who stood in need of redemption, there would have been no necessity for the Word of God to become man. And if the Word had not been made flesh, we should not have Mary as the Mother of God, because this privilege has its sole foundation in the necessity, determined by divine choice, to have God become man for the redemption of the human race. Sin, therefore, has become, if not the cause, at least the occasion of Mary's dignity.

Thus we plead with the Church: "Pray for us, sinners, now and in the hour of our death." The petition is twofold: we pray for help *now*, that means for each moment of our life; and at the hour of death, when we need the special grace of final perseverance. Our Lady will obtain for us both graces, since she received, what Dom Marmion so beautifully calls, "the grace of maternity toward Christ's mystical body." It was in the womb of His Blessed Mother that our Lord wedded the human race and became one body with it; that humanity could be restored to its original justice and favor with God. No one can come to the Father but through the Son. Neither will anyone be able to reach the Son, but through the Mother. For the miraculous conception and birth of our Lord from the womb of His Virgin Mother are and will remain the model and the basis of the mysterious conception and birth of Christ in the Church of Christ.

CHAPTER 37

COMFORTER OF THE AFFLICTED

Suffering makes a soul either bitter or better. The truth of this statement is evident to those who have a clear perception of the nature of suffering. In final analysis, pain and affliction are conditioned by love: either by exaggerated self-love, in which case pain eats into the heart and poisons the soul; or by love of God, in which instance suffering becomes our greatest single means of perfection.

The measure of happiness is determined by our ego, and has in most instances a direct relation to our personal comfort. There is little that grieves most of us, except the things that wound the body, our vanity, or our pride. We suffer also from man's ingratitude, mostly because it slights our calculated kindness. We are distressed by afflictions of other members of the family, not infrequently because such trials have a tendency to ruffle our daily routine. We likewise bewail the sorry plight of national or world affairs, mostly because such disorders affect us economically and give us a feeling of insecurity. With a positive disregard of reality, we are made despondent by things that should affect us but little, or we grieve in a manner which does violence to our dignity as children of God. Seldom do sins figure among the principal fountains of grief, unless they are a source of confusion and cause personal embarrassment. In other words, we have little sorrow for our faults considered as offenses against God. In theory we admit that sin is the greatest of all evils, since it directly affects the soul and its faculties, and because it is the cause of the disorders which we deplore in society. Yet, in spite of the fact that by our sins we contribute to the fundamental disorder of our souls, and to the confusing chaos of the world, we still fail to realize the sorrow which actual sin should produce. Our superficiality in matters spiritual, our inconstancy in directing our thoughts to God prevent us from seeing the real evil of sin, precisely because sin strikes so deep, and cannot be measured by those who live on the surface. In its manner of ravaging souls and society, sin is like one of those diseases which attack vital but hidden organs, and which remain unknown to the sufferer even while the sickness is nearing a crisis. Happy those souls who experience true sorrow at the thought of their sins, for only grace can produce this sorrow. Such sorrow is a product of love and places sin in right focus, namely as the only thing in creation which is incongruous, which harms God's majesty and His immense holiness, and would destroy Him, if that were possible. While the Stations of the Cross give us a remote understanding of the hideousness of sin, which thrice felled our Lord under its burden and ultimately contrived to hang Him between heaven and earth, they also furnish us with the most eloquent example of true sorrow for sin in the person of the Blessed Mother, who, grief-stricken, followed the Savior and stood beneath the Cross while her Son was crucified. No one can measure the billows of sorrow which flooded the heart of Mary at that moment, nor can anyone sound the depth of love which prompted her to suffer so much for sin and sinners.

Incidentally, this co-redeeming suffering of Our Lady has established her firmly in the role of comforter of the afflicted. Distress and pain are bound up with Christ's suffering in one way or the other. Suffering either has its origin in sin, or makes us participate and share in Christ's expiation. On both counts our crosses are the lengthening shadow of the Cross of Calvary. When they are received in the manner in which Christ accepted His Cross, they fully answer the same purpose for which Christ embraced His, and bring about the same effect. It is Mary's consoling task to teach us the true meaning of suffering in union with our Lord. While she alleviates our pain by her presence, she enables us to sanctify our distress in this holy manner, for the greatest blessing a Christian can obtain on earth is to labor with Christ, and to share in a measure His ultimate mission.

Many striking examples of Mary's direct help given to those who suffer, are recorded in the annals of hagiography. We quote an example, as it appeared in the diary of a Rumanian priest who was imprisoned during the present persecution. The report is taken from a recent issue of *Time*.

"I reached my prison on the afternoon of the day of my arrest. How long ago that was, how many days have passed, I do not know, because I am always in the dark. On that day, in complete darkness, I was led to this cell. When the door closed behind me, through God's mercy, I was thinking of God, and remembered to offer up my troubles for His glory, so that my humiliation was filled with God's own glory and became an immediate comfort to my soul.

"I tried then to get to know something of the place in which I was. I was already aware of much dampness and of a smell of human excrement. Guided by my nose, I drew as far away as possible from the place which I later learned was the location where the drains of five lavatories of the guards on five floors above me emptied themselves.

"I thought with horror that sometimes it is easier to resist actual pain and bodily wounds than the wave of sickness that assails one's stomach at a foul smell. I dreaded the possibility that I might weaken, and through God's mercy I was able to concentrate upon God, and it pleased God to fill my cell with an infinitesimal but overbrimming small part of His great glory.

"Feeling with my hands, after a long time I found two boards. They were damp, but they were whole, and they became my bed. They were about three feet long. I was able at first to get little sleep because rats kept scurrying over me. I have always been a friend of small animals, but the thought of rats kept me from sleeping, so I passed unforgettable moments of intimate union with the crucifix, which I conjured up before my mind. My own had been removed at the prison gates.

"Believe me, all of you who are outside, there is a phase of the cross which cannot be apprehended save by those who lie in jail. There is a part of the living God, which is only known to those who are themselves hidden in some subterranean cell, in darkness and in chains. There may be happiness in the light which streams through a small barred window of an above-ground prison cell, but God's happiness rests longer upon those who have not light's distraction.

"God, in His mercy, beat at my door, and the All Highest entered without keys. I recite the Rosary—the Glorious Mysteries—and I know our Lady is a comforter of the afflicted, and often my lips cannot form the words because my heart is overfull . . .

"Then I remember that I must not grow lax, and I pray for the union of all Rumanians; I pray that through my suffering I may be the subterranean mine which blows up the wall of division between Rumanians, so that all shall be brothers, and the Church shall be freed."

Do we not hear a distinct echo of Paul's words, who, himself in chains at Rome, wrote to the Colossians: "I rejoice now in the sufferings I bear for your sake; and what is lacking of the sufferings of Christ I fill up in my flesh, for His body, which is the Church" (Col. 1:24).

In the same Christian spirit Pius XII advised the people of Russia to turn to their Blessed Mother, the Comforter of the Afflicted. "We know that there are very many among you who still preserve their Christian faith within the innermost sanctuary of their conscience, who in no way allow themselves to be induced to help the enemies of religion, and whose ardent desire is to profess Christian teaching not only in private but if possible also openly, as becomes free men. We also know, and this knowledge has filled our heart with hope and with deepest comfort, that you love and honor the Virgin Mother of God with ardent affection, and that you venerate her sacred images. It is known that in the Kremlin itself there was constructed a church—today unfortunately no longer used for divine worship—dedicated to Our Lady assumed into heaven. This is a most clear testimony of the affectionate devotion which your parents and you have for the beloved Mother of God. . . . She is in fact the most loving and the most powerful Mother, and never was it heard that anyone had recourse to her and did not experience her protection. Continue, therefore, to venerate her with fervent piety, to love her ardently, and to invoke her with these words which you have been accustomed to address to her: To you alone has it been given, O holy and most pure Mother of God, to have your prayers heard without fail."

CHAPTER 38

HELP OF CHRISTIANS

Together with the immediately preceding titles, the present one completes the doctrine of Mary's universal mediation in its practical application. This universal mediation extends to the entire work of our salvation from beginning to end, and includes the first grace of conversion as well as the grace of final perseverance. Nor is this mediation exclusively individual. It extends to whole peoples as well. This is of particular interest to us who, as citizens of a country which is dedicated to Our Lady, claim her special protection.

Ever since Christopher Columbus set foot on the island of San Salvador in the West Indies on October 12, 1492, Mary has shown her predilection for the newly discovered lands of the Western Hemisphere. Nor was her name unsung in these regions even before Columbus' arrival. The famous Kensington Stone which was discovered in Minnesota in the year 1898, reveals conclusively that the Norsemen discovered America and penetrated to the very heart of this continent as far back as the year 1362, and left a memorial of their unquestionable faith and confidence in Mary, inscribing on the stone this prayer: "Hail Virgin Mary, save us from evil."

Less than forty years after Columbus landed on San Salvador, Our Lady appeared to the Aztec Indian, Juan Diego, on the hill of Tepeyac, three miles northeast of Mexico City, where today she is honored under the title of

Our Lady of Guadalupe. It may be well to remember that, when Our Lady appeared to Juan Diego in 1531, the English had not yet been settled in North America, and, because of the Line of Demarcation, the Spanish considered all of this territory their rightful dominion. Later the Spaniards actually settled in regions comprising about one-third of the present United States, which, together with Mexico, then carried the name of New Spain. To all of this territory the patronage of Our Lady of Guadalupe was officially decreed, declared, and commanded by the official representative of the Spanish Crown in the year 1746, a measure which was apostolically approved by Benedict XIV, in 1754.

While the Spanish throughout the solid south, and the French from Canada down to the Mississippi Valley, were eagerly claiming the largest part of our country and spreading the Catholic religion with its characteristic devotion to Mary, the English settled the thirteen colonies along the eastern seaboard. The Puritans who settled in New England, and the Anglicans who populated the southern colonies, had little love for one another. But one thing they shared—they both feared, hated, and persecuted Catholics. Out of this persecution came a colony founded as a refuge for English Catholics. It was the first Catholic colonization in the Western Hemisphere, under a charter issued by Charles I of England, on June 20, 1632, to Cecilius Calvert, the second Lord Baltimore. The new colony was named Maryland, ostensibly after Queen Henrietta Maria, but the real intent of the colonists was shown by the fact that they named their first settlement St. Mary's. The grant was furiously contested before the English Court, because it was a grant to a Catholic nobleman for the purpose of establishing a Catholic colony, but the committee of the Privy Council ultimately decided "to leave the Lord Baltimore to his charter, and the Protestants to their remedy at law." Since there was no such remedy, the decision stood firmly in favor of the first Lord Proprietary of the Province of Maryland.

It must interest American Catholics to recall that a patronage of Mary, similar to that established in Mexico in 1746, was declared specifically for this country just a century later. The Baltimore Council of 1846 chose Our Lady, under the title of Immaculate Conception, as Patroness of the United States. There was some slight hesitation on the part of a few members of the hierarchy, because the Immaculate Conception was not yet declared a dogma of the Church. It was felt, however, that the honor to Mary would be greater if they did not await the formal definition of the dogma. Pope Pius IX graciously approved the choice of the American Bishops, eight years before he proclaimed the dogma of the Immaculate Conception.

Under the protection of the Immaculate Conception the Church in the United States has continued to prosper. Not quite as marvelously as in Mexico, where the Church gained some ten million members within the first ten years after Our Lady's apparition at Guadalupe, yet the growth of the Church in our country has been steady and healthy, so that Catholics at present form at least one-sixth of our population and are the largest, single religious body in the nation.

The influence of the Blessed Virgin has been strikingly evident in the history of both Americas, and more particularly in the history of the United States. Among the most recent signs are the dates connected with American participation in World War II. Pearl Harbor was bombed on December 7, 1941, which was the vigil of the Feast of the Immaculate Conception. Congress declared war on December 8, the day of the feast itself. The war ended on August 14, 1945, vigil of the Feast of the Assumption of the

Blessed Mother in our part of the world. In Japan, where the decision to surrender was made, this was August 15, the feastday proper. Such things can be called coincidences, but even as coincidences they are very striking. They remind us that our Mother and our Patron is watching over us and protecting us from on high.

History records that Pope St. Pius V originated the title of Our Lady, Help of Christians, in gratitude for the victory of Lepanto, where the combined Papal, Spanish, Venetian, and Genoese fleets, under the command of Don Juan of Austria, gained a decisive victory over the Turkish fleet, on October 7, 1571. The sixth lesson of the Roman Breviary for the feast of Our Lady of Help confirms this tradition. Since the title was already used in the first printed copy of the Litany known as the Dillingen text, which seems to have been published in the year 1558, it is more probable that Pius V inserted this ancient title permanently into the Litany and decreed its universal use in commemoration of the above victory.

CHAPTER 39

QUEEN OF ANGELS

To bring out the full import of this title, as well as of the remaining invocations of the Litany, we must first establish Mary's absolute claim to the title of Queen. It should be recalled at this place that God alone has universal kingship over all things by virtue of His essence; He governs all things in creation and directs them to their final end. Our thesis, therefore, is designed to prove the double proposition: that Jesus possesses this title by essence, and that our Lady shares in the universal kingship of Christ by participation.

It is a matter of faith that Christ, because of His divine personality, is in His human nature the universal King of creation. This doctrine is well established by our Lord Himself, who claimed all power in heaven and on earth (Matt. 28:18). This accords with the words of the Apocalypse: "I am the Alpha and the Omega, the first and the last, the beginning and the end" (Apoc. 22:13). St. Paul is no less explicit when he says: "All things have been created through and unto Him, and He is before all creatures, and in Him all things hold together" (Col. 1:16–17). By His hypostatic union with a created nature, He is become the Head of all creation, and from Him creation receives its ultimate and most august consecration. This kingship Christ proclaimed before Pilate, but He then added that His kingdom was not of this world. His kingdom was spiritual, the kingdom of God, opposed to the kingdom of Satan. Christ had come into the world that we might have life and have it more abundantly, transferring us from the slavery of the powers of darkness into His kingdom; making us partakers of the lot of the saints in light.

Pius XI sanctioned the feast of Christ the King for the universal Church on the last Sunday of October, in the year 1925.

Can it be said that Our Lady shares in Christ's universal kingship in the sense that she is Queen of all creatures in subordination to our Lord? We have a strong argument of tradition in favor of this assertion, since the Fathers of both East and West refer to her repeatedly under this title. Roman as well as Oriental liturgies proclaim Mary, Queen of the heavens, Queen of the world. Among the mysteries of the Rosary, commonly recited in the Church since the thirteenth century, the last of all is that of the crowning of Our Lady in heaven.

Theological arguments are not less conclusive. Jesus Christ is King of the universe, even as man, in virtue of His divine personality. But Mary, Mother of God made man, shares in the dignity of her Son. Nor can it be objected that the mother of a king is not by that simple fact queen in the strict sense of the term. Mary is the Mother of Him who from the first instant of His conception is King of the universe, because of the hypostatic union of His divine and human nature. Mary herself belongs to the hypostatic order, since the personality of Christ is the term of her divine motherhood. Hence, as Father Merkelbach remarks, she shares connaturally, as Mother of God, in His universal kingship. Besides, Our Lady was associated closely with the victory of Christ over sin, Satan, and death, by which He acquired a second claim on universal kingship, which He already possessed as Son of God, by right of conquest.

Following are some of the consequences which this proposition implies. As universal king Christ has power to establish and promulgate the New Law, which, as St. Thomas says, is engraved in our hearts by grace, according to the words of Jeremias: "Behold the days shall come, says the Lord, and I will make a new covenant with the house of Israel, and with the house of Juda. I will give My law in their bowels, and I will write it in their hearts" (Jer. 31:31–33). But, Mary is the dispenser of all graces which are imprinted on our minds, hearts, and wills, in a hidden and interior manner, in so far as she has merited them with and in dependence on our Lord.

Even though Mary shares in our Lord's legislative and

dominative powers by means of grace, she does not seem to have a part in His judicial power, which is His explicitly, since God has appointed Him Judge of the living and the dead (Acts 10:42). "For the Father does not judge any man, but all judgment has been given to the Son, that all men may honor the Son even as they honor the Father" (John 5:22–23). Tradition calls Our Lady not the Mother of justice, but the Mother of mercy, according to the words of the *Salve Regina:* "Hail Holy Queen, Mother of Mercy."

Our Lady exercises her queenship both on earth and in heaven. On earth it is spiritual and supernatural rather than temporal and natural, although it extends in a secondary manner to temporal affairs inasmuch as they are related to salvation and sanctification. In heaven the essential glory of the blessed depends on Jesus' merits and hers, while she contributes to the accidental glory of both angels and saints, as Father Garrigou-Lagrange remarks, by the light she communicates to them, and by the joy they have in her presence, and in the realization of what she does for souls. To both she also manifests Christ's plan for the extension of His kingdom.

Her queenship extends to purgatory, for she prompts the faithful on earth to pray for the souls detained there, while she herself offers their prayers to God, thereby increasing their value. It even extends to the demons in hell, who are obliged to recognize Our Lady's power. She can make their temptations cease, can save souls from their snares, and can repulse their attacks. "The demons suffer more," says St. Grignon de Montfort, "from being conquered by the humility of Mary than by the omnipotence of God."

When we come to Mary's specific title of Queen of Angels, we see once again that her queenship is dependent on the kingship of her Son, which is absolute, according to the words of St. Paul: "He is the image of the invisible God, the firstborn of every creature. For in Him were created all things in the heavens and on the earth, things visible and invisible, whether Thrones, or Dominations, or Principalities, or Powers" (Col. 1:15–16). Mary's royalty is one of participation, but even as such it is a marvel to the angels, as St. Thomas says in substance: "Though the angels do not manifest special respect for men, being their superiors by nature and living in holy intimacy with God, yet the Archangel Gabriel, when saluting Mary, showed himself full of veneration for her. He understood that she was far above him through her fullness of grace, her intimacy with God, and her perfect purity."

Mary is Queen of the Angels, since her mission is higher than theirs. They are servants, whereas she is the Mother of God. Her dignity surpasses that of all saints and angels, as Pius IX says in his Bull on the Immaculate Conception: "Drawing from the treasures of His divinity, God endowed her, more than all angels and saints, with such an abundance of heavenly gifts that, all beautiful and perfect, she appeared in such a plenitude of innocence and holiness that, except God's, no greater than hers can be conceived, and that no mind, but the mind of God, can measure it."

While Mary contributes to the accidental glory of the angels, what are we to say of their essential glory? Does the essential glory of the angels, like that of the saints, also directly depend on Christ, and thus indirectly on Mary?

Here we are confronted with the text of St. Paul, who states that it was the mystery of God's will and His good pleasure to be dispensed in the fullness of time "to re-establish all things in Christ, both those in the heavens and those on the earth" (Eph. 1:10). Our Lord is not the Redeemer of the Angels, as He is the Redeemer of the human race. The angels were not to recover lost grace through Christ. The good angels had always possessed it. The evil spirits could never recover it throughout eternity. Yet, would it be too much to say that God from all eternity had preordained that sin was to find its ultimate vindication in Christ; that the good angels who cooperated with the grace of God, received this grace in anticipation of the merits of Jesus Christ; and that even the essential happiness of the angels was to receive its adorning crown and its final consecration from our Lord, the firstborn of all creatures, the King of Angels, and thus indirectly from Mary, their Queen? Is it not eminently suited to the dignity of the God-man and to that of the angels that they, too, should be included in some mysterious way in the all-embracing plan of God, who conceived Christ as both the end and the beginning of the way mapped out at the creation of the universe? Was not all to center in Christ, the universal King? This would give a new insight into the origin and the frightful malice of the sin of the angels, and encompass it in its entire profundity. Father Scheeben remarks: "We apprehend the basic reason why God could allow the angels to fall, and why He could permit all mankind to fall through their instigation: because He not only knew that the havoc thus wrought would be repaired, but wished to utilize it for the supreme revelation of His goodness and glory. Indeed, the revelation of God's glory and love reached its peak in the employment of sin as an instrument, so to speak, for the attainment of its ends. By the very fact that Christ satisfied for sin, God's honor was not merely saved, but was further glorified according to a new aspect. This is all the more true when it compelled sin in the midst of its supreme triumph to take part in the conquest of itself. Sin celebrated its triumph when it strove and actually contrived to slay God's Anointed. But at the very moment that Christ seemed to succumb to it, He performed the supreme act of adoration and glorification of God. That act did more than merely compensate for sin. It drew the most precious honey from the poison of its sting, forced sin to achieve an effect opposite to its intention, and deeply humiliated sin in a way that not even the everlasting punishment of hell could equal, thereby securing for God a triumph that would have been impossible without sin." It would seem a pity to apply this only to the sin of humanity which, in final instance, was the "mystery of iniquity" of which St. Paul speaks, as it descended from angels to men; and thus exclude the good angels from this added glory of having their victory associated with Christ. Since this is also part of the mysterious doctrine of the Incarnation, Mary's part in it becomes likewise evident, and we may once again realize why the angels welcome Our Lady as their Queen and Mistress.

Here we add, as a final consideration, that the whole angelic creation seeks to accomplish the one purpose of creation at large, namely to secure God's glory. The angels, always enjoying God's presence and His adorable beauty, have no thought other than to please and to glorify God in all their actions. But the glorification of God by any angel, and indeed by all the angels together, is only finite. Their essential office of serving and praising God must be integrated with that of Christ, who alone glorifies God in an infinite manner. In this respect Christ's example becomes the norm, standard, and model, after which the angel's conduct is fashioned, and by which the angel attains his final end. This is beautifully expressed in the Preface of the Mass where it is said that "through Jesus Christ, our Lord, angels praise God's majesty, Dominations adore it, and Powers tremble." Mary's participation in this absolute rule is indirect, relative to the dominion of our Lord, but for that matter, no less necessary and essential, because of her divine maternity.

Pius IX asserts that, according to the Fathers, Mary is higher by grace than even the cherubim and seraphim, and the whole heavenly host combined. On the strength of the preceding consideration this statement appears in a new light. The cherubim shine with the splendor of their knowledge. But Our Lady has penetrated into the divine mysteries deeper than they, particularly in the mysteries of the Incarnation and the Redemption, in which she took an active part. The seraphim burn with the flame of love; but more ardent still is the living flame of Mary's love for God, who enabled her in His indescribable mercy to participate even in the final glorification of the angels.

CHAPTER 40

QUEEN OF PATRIARCHS

The name "Patriarch" according to its etymological derivation, indicates the father or chief of a race. The term is applied to the antediluvian fathers, as well as to the three great ancestors of Israel: Abraham, Isaac, and Jacob. In the New Testament the name is extended to the twelve sons of Jacob (Acts 7:8) and to King David (Acts 2:29). But it belongs first and foremost to Adam, the progenitor of them all, and the father of the human race in general.

That Mary, as a natural descendant of Adam, excelled

her illustrious forebear, is well established by the dogmatic definition of her Immaculate Conception. When this privilege is considered in its full weight and consequence it is clear that Our Lady was not only preserved immune from all stain of original sin—an exemption which placed her on a level with Adam in his state of original justice—but also was established in a supernatural state of holiness which guaranteed her absolute freedom from sin. In this she is placed far above Adam. In contrast with Adam, who, although endowed with the extraordinary prerogatives which sanctifying grace and the gift of integrity implied, was still able to choose against his better judgment, Mary was confirmed in grace by special assistance of divine Providence, in such a manner that all possibility of choosing against her better judgment was totally eliminated. Nor did this privilege interfere with, or dwarf in any way her liberty or the use of her free will. Her privilege in effect was intended to preserve and to confirm her full liberty in the order of moral goodness, as a faithful and most pure image of God's own liberty, which is at once sovereign and incapable of sin. This special privilege was granted to Mary only in and because of her Son. As the Redeemer of the human race our Lord could not allow the least possibility of stain of sin in His own Mother, as St. Augustine says: "For the honor of her Son, who came to remit the sins of the world, Mary is never included when there is question of sin." More than that. In union with Christ Mary repaired the harm done by Adam, and effectively brought about the salvation of the human race. By furnishing our Lord and Savior with His mortal flesh, in which He could suffer and die, Mary took an integral part in the work of Christ's redemption. It was her mission, with Christ, to defeat sin, and to become the principle of the continued restoration and firm foundation of holiness which was lost by our first parents. In other words, Our Lady was created as a daughter of Adam for the sole reason that she was destined to be the Mother of the Redeemer, to whom she would give His human nature. Consequently, her bodily relation to Adam was entirely subservient to her bodily relation to Christ. All this is contained in the text of the Protogospel (Gen. 3:15) which predicted a victorious enmity against the devil and sin, as effected by the Woman and her seed.

The question has been raised why Our Blessed Lady was not immune from pain and death, though these are generally considered natural consequences of original sin. The answer is that with her the same reasons prevail which prompted our Lord to accept them. Pain and death are not primarily consequences of original sin. They are rather the natural result of the animal condition of human nature which, of itself, and like animal nature in general, is subject to pain and corruption of the body. It was a special privilege that Adam was exempt from these consequences in the state of innocence, and the removal of this grace returned him to his original condition. When Jesus willingly accepted suffering and death, He did so freely for love of us, while Mary accepted the same in imitation of her divine Son, and in order to unite herself to Him in the work of redemption. They could thus choose because suffering and death, being directly a result of the passibility of human nature, are only indirectly a punishment for original sin.

That Mary was absolutely preserved from rampant concupiscence and darkness of understanding, is clearly evidenced in the fact that these disorders can be viewed only as punishments. By nature man moves spontaneously from

within, since he knows intellectually supra-sensible existence and truth, and is freely drawn toward rational good.
His mental capacity is such that he can acquire knowledge,
both natural and, in a measure, supernatural, according
to certain psychological laws, without the direct interference of God. The same is true in regard to control of the
passions. The flesh wars against the spirit, and the spirit
against the flesh, as the Apostle remarks, but to establish
peace and harmony between the two, reason and will are
the God-given faculties which, under normal conditions,
should suffice to keep both under control. When Adam
could no longer regulate his passions in an absolute manner, and found his intellect badly darkened, he suffered
these spiritual handicaps in direct punishment of his guilty
act. Our Lady's mind, however, free from original sin and
its baneful consequences, was never subject to error or illusion, nor was there at any time any disordered movement
of her sensitive nature. In other words, there was always
perfect order, and no possible escape of her sensibility
from the control of reason and will.

Instead of searching for some possible disorder in the
sensitive nature of Mary, we should realize that her sensibility was of a perfection unknown to any other child of
Adam, and thus her capacity of suffering was more intense.
Moreover, Mary was more sensitive to the real cause of
suffering, namely to sin in all its ugly aspects. Because Our
Lady was so pure, her heart so consumed by love of God,
she suffered for our sins pain out of all proportion, precisely because sin is out of all proportion. Thus Mary's
Immaculate Conception, far from alleviating pain and
suffering, made her capable of suffering more intensely,
while it disposed her to bear pain more heroically.

Mary's charity was greater from the first moment of her

conception than that of Adam in the state of innocence. This seems well established by the words of Pius IX, who says that our Lord, drawing from the treasure of His divinity, made Mary all beautiful and perfect, which made her appear in such a plenitude of innocence and holiness that, except God's, no greater than hers can be conceived, and that no mind, but the mind of God, can measure it. Sanctity in a soul, like grace, is the effect of uncreated love and is proportionate to it. As St. Thomas says: "God loves one more than another by the fact that He wills him a higher good." Now the highest good that our Lord can wish to any of His creatures is to select one to be His Mother. Or, in the words of Bossuet: "Our Lord loved Mary as His Mother, and considered her as such from the moment she was conceived."

In consequence of this Our Lady's obedience to the will of God was especially in vivid contrast to the disobedience of her first parent who brought sin into the world, and by sin death. Mary, on the contrary, is our life, our sweetness, and our hope, who by an act of perfect obedience came to participate in the most perfect act of supreme obedience of her Son, of whom we read: "In the head of the book it is written of Me that I should do Thy will: O My God, I have desired it, and Thy law is in the midst of My heart" (Ps. 39:8-9).

Finally, Mary attained to an intimacy with God which was by far greater than that Adam enjoyed during his happy days in Paradise. Sacred Scripture suggests a very close and intimate commerce between God and our first parents, but nothing that could equal the intimacy of Father and Daughter, of Mother and Son, or the intimacy which existed between the Holy Spirit of God and God's chosen Bride.

When the matter is viewed from the standpoint of Mary's universal mediation, it is at once evident that Adam's conversion and final perseverance in the grace of God have been dependent, like all created grace, on Our Lady's intervention and, as such, Mary deserves the name of Queen of Patriarchs with as much right as she bears the name of Queen of Angels, and all the other titles of her Litany.

CHAPTER 41

QUEEN OF PROPHETS

The prophet of the Old Testament was not merely a man enlightened by God to forecast future events. He was an interpreter, and a messenger supernaturally commissioned to communicate God's will and designs to the Chosen People. He was to preserve and develop the knowledge and practice of the Old Law, to lead God's people back when they had strayed, and gradually to prepare the way for the new kingdom of God which the Messiah was to establish on earth.

The list of prophets during the Old Dispensation is long and impressive. It begins with Abraham, who is the first mentioned in Sacred Scripture as being favored with divine communications, the friend of God to whom the promises were made, and to his seed, that he should be heir of the world (Rom. 4:13). The line continues down to Malachias, who predicted the reprobation of the Jews and the calling of the Gentiles. In the time of the Machabees prophets no longer appeared. Religious revelation and the moral code expressed in the Sacred Writings were full and clear. Scribes and doctors of the Law replaced the prophets as guides of the populace, and the people awaited the fulfillment of the promises and the coming of the Messiah, who was to be the crown and the consummation of all prophecies.

At the break of the Messianic era there appeared Elizabeth and Zachary, when Our Lady was already with child, and, shortly after, Simeon and Anna, when Jesus was presented in the temple. John the Baptist immediately preceded Christ, preaching in the desert of Judea, and saying: "Repent, for the kingdom of heaven is at hand" (Matt. 3:2). Then came the Messiah in person, long awaited as *The Prophet* (Deut. 18:15), who unlike His predecessors spoke from within, and revealed of the Father with an authority hitherto unknown.

Even the early Church knew its prophets, since prophecy was then one of the principal charismata, conferred abundantly "for edification, and encouragement, and consolation" (I Cor. 14:3). The list of prophets closed with St. John, the apostle, who wrote his Apocalypse as a prophetic account of the struggles and victories of the new kingdom, as man awaits the last return of his Lord and Maker, at the consummation of time.

Our Blessed Lady is called Queen of Prophets because all the Messianic prophecies of the Old Testament, while they deal directly with the coming and the essential life-work of the Messiah, indirectly relate to Mary as the Mother of Jesus. A few prophecies immediately refer to Our Lady in such words as those of Isaias: "Behold a virgin shall conceive, and bear a Son, and His name shall be called Emmanuel" (Is. 7:14). In the Protogospel of Genesis Mary was thus represented as the Mother of the Redeemer and the divinely chosen instrument in and by whom Christ would crush the head of the serpent. Together these two prophecies form the classic foundation of the established Catholic doctrine that she was one with our Lord in the work of redemption. Christ is pictured as the new Adam, who made use of Mary as the second Eve, in order to re-create the world and renew the face of the earth. In her dignity, virtue, and activity, Mary prefigures the grace of redemption to be distributed to all. In other words: Mary, the spiritual mother of each individually redeemed soul, is the model of the divine filiation of grace of redeemed persons. "Therefore," says St. Bernard, "all generations call her blessed, the Mother of God, the Mistress of the world, who has given life and glory to all generations. For in her the just find grace, and the sinners forgiveness. De-servedly the eyes of all creatures are turned toward her, because in her, by her, and from her, the benign hand of God re-created that which He had created." It is thus that the prophets saw the Messiah as King of the Universe, according to the words of Isaias: "A Child is born to us, and a Son is given to us, and the government is upon His shoulders" (Is. 9:7); while they saw Our Lady as His Mother, the second Mother of all the living, who presides over her inheritance as the Queen of the New Creation in Christ.

Aside from these direct and formal prophecies about Our Lady, the Church has used a great many references from the Old Testament, particularly from the Sapiential Books. The application of these texts is formal testimony that the Church considers Mary so closely related to Wis-dom personified that she feels entitled to apply these texts to her in an entirely unique manner. It can be accepted on the strength of the authority of the Church, that the application of these texts to Mary has been the intention of the Holy Spirit.

According to this explanation, is it stretching the truth to speak of an indirect and remote inspiration of the prophets in some mysterious way by means of Mary? Does not the Church indicate that she was before God's mind from all eternity, "playing before Him at all times" (Prov. 8:30)? If the saints of the Old Testament were entirely governed by the future merits of Jesus Christ, may we not speak in like manner of a participation in the future merits of Mary, who, although a subordinate factor in the universal plan of redemption, was a real factor indeed. It seems not unlikely that the Church would allow us to apply the words of Holy Scripture to Mary in this sense, since she repeats with the Prophet: "Let thy dwelling be in Jacob, and thy inheritance in Israel, and take root in My elect" (Ecclus. 24:14). And again: "I will pour forth doctrine as prophecy, and leave it to them that seek wisdom, and will not cease to instruct their offspring even to the holy age" (Ecclus. 24:46).

In fine, Mary was a prophetess in her own right, when she predicted about herself in the *Magnificat:* "Henceforth all generations shall call me blessed" (Luke 1:48). This prophecy has found continual fulfillment for nearly two thousand years. Some authors seem to belittle Mary's song of praise, because of the lack of originality in its references to known places of Sacred Scripture. However, this rather emphasizes the fact that Our Lady knew these Messianic prophecies so well that she at once saw their fulfillment in the light of divine revelation, just as Elizabeth had seen that through the fruit of Mary's womb God was beginning to bless men through His Mother. As the Queen of Prophets Mary had a profound understanding of these mysteries of God, which she herself was to live. As the eternal covenant between God and His people, who raises the earth to its supernatural height, and possesses the inheritances that were destroyed, she will be the joy of all future generations who are blessed with her in the fulfillment of these prophecies.

CHAPTER 42

QUEEN OF APOSTLES

The name of apostle was given to twelve selected disciples of Christ, as we know from the words of St. Luke: "Now it came to pass in those days, that He went out to the mountain to pray, and continued all night in prayer to God. And when day broke, He summoned His disciples; and from those He chose twelve, whom He also named Apostles" (Luke 6:12–13). The origin of the apostolate lies therefore in a special vocation, a formal appointment of the Lord to a determined office, with connected authority and duties. In order to fill this office it seems to have been necessary to be trained by Jesus, and to have seen the Risen Lord. At least these were the conditions required by the apostles themselves in the candidate for the place of Judas Iscariot, as we read in the Acts: "Therefore, of these men who have been in our company all the time that the Lord Jesus moved among us, from John's baptism until the day that He was taken up from us, of these one must become a witness with us of His resurrection" (Acts 1:21–22).

Saul of Tarsus, miraculously converted and called to preach the Gospel to the Gentiles, claimed this title with much insistency and its rights on similar grounds, namely, that he had seen the Lord after His resurrection, and had been instructed by Jesus Himself, as he said: "Have I not seen Jesus our Lord? Do I speak these things on human authority?" (I Cor. 9:1; 8)

Yet, in view of the personal instruction which the apostles had received from our Lord, regardless of the many miracles which they had witnessed, we are struck with amazement to see them so little enlightened, even after the Resurrection. Christ had to upbraid them for their lack of faith and hardness of heart, in that they had not believed those who had seen Him after He was risen (Mark 16:14). Even at the moment that He was leaving them to go to the Father, they inquired whether at this time He would restore the kingdom to Israel (Acts 1:6). It took no less than the Pentecostal fires to enlighten their slow minds and open their hearts to the great revelation of the Holy Spirit. Then only did they fully and entirely grasp that, day after day, they had lived on familiar terms with the Messiah, the Son of God, the Desired of nations, the Redeemer of Israel, who had been foretold by the prophets.

On the day of Pentecost they must have turned with profound respect and tender veneration to Mary, who presided over them in silence, though yielding the place of honor to Peter (Acts 1:13–14). It was at this occasion, Father Mateo remarks, that they realized their former blindness in regard to the lessons taught by the miracles of Jesus, and the lessons which were to be learned from the silence and modesty of His Mother. From that hour on, she became the living oracle of the secrets of God and, before the apostles dispersed to spread the gospel of the New

Kingdom, they must have often gathered round the Mother of Jesus, plying her with questions, begging to be told the secrets which she kept hidden in her heart. Conscious that a great part of that treasure belonged by right to the infant Church, Mary, modestly, tenderly, and with great wisdom, must have expounded to the astonished apostles what she alone knew. Thus the apostles and the evangelists learned many things which, but for Mary, no one could have ever known or even guessed; as, for instance, the mystery of the Annunciation and the virgin birth, of the Incarnation at Bethlehem with its surrounding heavenly pageantry, of the flight to Egypt, as well as the other details of Christ's hidden life, particularly of the happenings in Jerusalem when the Lord Jesus, as a twelve-year-old boy, went up to the Temple. St. Ambrose remarks that it is not strange that St. John should have spoken better of the mystery of the Incarnation than the others did, for he lived at the source of heavenly secrets, inasmuch as he lived in Our Lady's company when he wrote the fourth Gospel.

Father Delbrel deftly remarks that the great work of our Lord's public life was the training of the Twelve. In this Christ employed most of His time; it was, so to speak, His habitual occupation. Preaching to the crowds was merely secondary, and was to serve as a model of what the preaching of His disciples should be. The truth of these words is well borne out by the actual facts. For, when our Lord left the earth there was no visible Church other than the nuclear group of about a hundred and twenty (Acts 1:15). It was only on Pentecost Sunday that people started to enter: "And on that day there were added about three thousand souls" (Acts 2:41). Mary was in the midst of all this spiritual activity, doing her share in silence. Her influence on the infant Church has been aptly compared to that of the heart, since it remains hidden, and since it was principally of the affective order—the influence of a mother. Her vocation was to contemplate and to love, and to obtain by her unceasing prayer the spread of the faith and the salvation of souls.

Indeed, after the departure of Jesus the apostles must have been very close to Mary's heart, inasmuch as they were the successors of Christ and filled with the plenitude of the priestly spirit, which is the spirit of her Son. Although lacking the priestly character herself, her dignity of Mother of God overshadowed that of ordained priests, for she had given them both the Priest and the Victim of the Sacrifice of the Cross—which she had offered herself with Him, an oblation which the apostles were called upon to perpetuate as the ministers of her Son. Thus Mary was truly their Queen; and not of them only, but of the others as well who were to share in the apostolate by subsequent calling, and who were to represent Jesus in His priestly character until the end of time.

Our Lord who has willed to have need of Mary in the work of salvation, has willed also to have need of priests, inasmuch as they are an integral part of the application of the redemption. It also seems evident that the formation of holy priests has been left to her special care. In this Jesus Himself gave the example. Thirty years of the life of the incarnate Word are summed up in these few words: "He was subject to them" (Luke 2:51). He who from the beginning was full of grace and truth has willed to submit Himself to His Mother, while, according to the law of progress, "He advanced in wisdom and age and grace before God and men" (Luke 2:52). Father Garrigou-Lagrange remarks:

Because of the work to which they are called, Mary is specially zealous for the sanctification of priests. She sees that they share in the priesthood of her Son, and she watches over their souls that the grace of their ordination may become a reality, that they grow into living images of the Savior. She loves them as sons of predilection, just as she loved St. John, who was committed to her on Calvary. She protects them against the dangers which surround them, and she attracts their hearts to herself in order to raise them up and to lead them to greater intimacy with her Son. She helps priests in a special way at the altar, so that they may become more fully conscious of their union with the Principal Offerer. She is spiritually present at the sacramental oblation which perpetuates the substance of the Sacrifice of the Cross, and she distributes to the priest the actual graces, that he may minister with recollection and in the spirit of self-immolation. Thus she helps the priest to share in Jesus' victimhood as well as in His priesthood in order to form him to the image of the Heart of her Son.

With Jesus Mary also plants priestly vocations and cultivates them. She knows that without priests there is no solemn baptism, no confession, no Mass, no Christian marriage, no extreme unction, in short, no Christian life. For which reason, those who desire the world to return to paganism war against the priests. Their primary aim is to destroy Catholic education in general, to close seminaries, and to persecute the ordained priesthood as a systematic procedure and with diabolical persistence. Since Mary "alone has overcome all heresies," both of a general and private nature, the priest, and likewise the seminarian, will do well to turn to Mary, and to erect his spiritual edifice on the strong foundation of a solid devotion to the Blessed Mother. Our Lady is the most lovable as well as the most loving of mothers; so she should be the most loved by those children of hers who are, in Christ, her first love. To resemble her is to resemble Jesus; to study her, is to study the greatest example, after Jesus, of all virtues; to love and imitate her, is to love and imitate her Son, whose most cherished devotion was and ever will be the devotion to His Blessed Mother.

CHAPTER 43

QUEEN OF MARTYRS

The original meaning of the word martyr, according to its Greek derivation, is that of a witness who gives testimony to a fact of which he has knowledge from personal observation. However, early in the first century of the Christian era the word received the added connotation of giving testimony to one's faith in Christ, at the risk of being forced either to give up one's convictions, or to expose oneself to the punishment of death. Thus St. Stephen was a witness who, early in the history of Christianity, sealed his testimony with his blood. Yet, it was only by degrees that the term martyr came to be exclusively applied to those who had actually died for the faith.

Little is known with absolute certainty about the approximate number of martyrs from the first persecution under Nero (64) until the time that Constantine established lasting peace (313). The general estimate reaches several millions, two millions of whom are buried under the streets of Rome.

The accounts of the tortures which the martyrs suffered

from the time they were arrested until brought to trial—
which was usually several months—read like the records
of a modern concentration camp such as Dachau or Buchen-
wald. They were thrown into dungeons where darkness
reigned supreme. Deprived of food, save enough to keep
them alive, of water and air; weighed down with chains or
placed in stocks; exposed to all manner of infection from
vermin, to heat, overcrowding, and the absence of anything like proper sanitation, only the stronger among them
could survive until their trial. After trial they were thrown
to the beasts, quartered or crucified as the case might be,
or stretched on the rack and their bodies torn apart with
iron rakes. Almost worse was the fate of those condemned
to penal servitude, who were doomed to pass the remainder
of their days in the darkness of salt mines, barely covered,
hungry, and exhausted, with no place to rest save the damp
ground.

It is easy to understand that they who suffered such
excruciations for the sanctity of their faith, were greatly
venerated by their friends who escaped torments. Their
example filled the other Christians with fear and love of
God, rather than with apprehension of possible martyrdom. It is in this spirit that Tertullian wrote, with the
ardor and the usual impetuosity of his nature: "There are
no witnesses to prove our crimes. Trajan ordered Pliny
not to seek us out, yet to punish us if we are known. What a
paralogism! The actual procedure is stranger yet. Instead
of being tortured until we confess, we are tortured until
we deny." Then, commenting on the number of Christians, he continues: "We are but of yesterday, still we fill
your cities, your towns, your councils, even the palace, the
senate, the forum. The only things we left to you are your
temples. But carry on, good officials, you will become much

better in the eyes of the people if you sacrifice the Christians. Crucify us, torture us, condemn us, destroy us! Your injustice is proof of our innocence. Your savage dealings accomplish nothing. We become more numerous every time you cut us down. The blood of martyrs is the seed of Christians."

This feeling of solidarity, along with spiritual fruitfulness, was in final analysis the strength of every martyr. They understood better than anyone what it meant to fill up the sufferings of Christ in their flesh for Christ's body, which is the Church (Col. 1:24). In this sense Christ had suffered and sacrificed, and it was their mystical consecration to receive death, not as a punishment or penal necessity, but rather as the inevitable testimony of their love for the honor of God and the benefit of all the faithful, much after the example and in the spirit and power of Christ. St. Augustine would explain it a few centuries later, when he commented on the words of the Prophet: "I will go into Thy house with burnt offerings" (Ps. 65:13). It was the martyr's privilege to join the Master in the perfect sacrifice, as a burnt offering, a holocaust. "What is a holocaust?" the Saint asks. "It is a whole victim burned up, but with divine fire. The parts of a sacrifice are one thing; a holocaust is another thing. When the whole is consumed by divine fire, it is called a holocaust." It is this spirit of offering which the martyrs brought to the place of martyrdom, as it brought Mary to the foot of the Cross. This is also the reason why they claim Mary as their Queen in suffering, for she shared more intensely and more intimately in Jesus' pains by her inner union with Him on the Cross, than did all the martyrs by their bodily affliction. This thought is brought out by the Church in the Feast of the Compassion of Our Lady, as well as in the Feast of the Seven Dolors. It is beautifully expressed in the *Stabat Mater:*

> Let me to my final breath,
> In my body bear the death
> Of that dying Son of Thine.

Our Lady, who formally became Queen of Martyrs beneath the Cross, remains so through the ages. She was thus honored during the first era of the Church; thus she remains, by divine dispensation, the faithful Queen of our modern martyrs. We cited an example of the Rumanian priest behind the Iron Curtain, who found lasting encouragement in praying his Rosary. We add a parallel incident from behind the Bamboo Curtain. Writes Father Madigan, a Maryknoll missioner, who has gone through the Communistic mill in Red China:

The Chinese Reds have demolished altars, converted churches into granaries, set up crucifixes as targets for shooting practice. They have hounded and persecuted Christians and have shocked them by sacrileges. The crosses and holy pictures that were not concealed, the Reds confiscated. The Chinese Christians today have little in the way of material representation of the God they adore. Little, save the tiny strands of twisted string, woven into rosaries. Easily made, easily concealed, the knotted string is in many places the last visible relic of a religion that only a few years ago was free and flourishing.

He recalls the last Christmas at Our Lady of Fatima Parish, where he was stationed shortly before the Reds intensified their persecution:

All afternoon on December 24, Christians trekked ten to twenty miles from their distant homes in the hills, to the central church. All afternoon one or more Communistic soldiers stood in front of, or in the church, watching, waiting, and silent. Men with Mausers over their shoulders were asked to step aside as the Christians decorated the walls and the ceiling. Men with tommy guns sat in the front pew as the altar was decked with colored cloth and flowers. Midnight Mass was celebrated before the largest congregation the church had ever held.

Before Mass there was a short but impressive ceremony. On fifteen banners hanging from a wire stretched across the sanctuary, were pictures representing the fifteen mysteries of the Rosary. My mission had exactly fifteen out-stations. Each station or community of Christians was dedicated to a Mystery of the Rosary, as special characteristics of the groups suggested. The village where Christianity was first introduced was dedicated to the Annunciation; one where many converts were made, to the Resurrection; one where Christians had suffered for the faith, to the Crucifixion.

As the name of each community was called, a representative approached the altar rail to stand before the respective banner on which was inscribed in Chinese characters the name of the Mystery of the Rosary, the name of the community dedicated to that special Mystery, and the date of its founding. Meanwhile the several hundred Christians in the nave of the church prayed the Litany.

Such simple, impressive ceremonies have long since been banned. Open profession of faith has become impossible under the Red all-out persecution. As a rule the Chinese are silent about the nature of their tortures and the burden of them, but when it comes to their devotion to Our Lady, they find it hard to hide it behind a mask of supernatural apathy. Of this, Father Madigan relates a striking instance, which happened during the last days of his relative freedom:

Risking the rage of the Communists, I visited the local jail to see one of my parishioners. They often tagged one, showing sympathy for a prisoner, with the same accusations as the one held. The official in charge jumped to his feet, furious at the presumptuous request. He delivered a ten-minute lecture for the benefit of the assembled onlookers about the evils of capitalism, the savagery of Americans, and the virtues of Mao and the Russians. But finally he yielded to my request, and opened the door of the prison cell—it had once been my bedroom— and called the prisoner. Looking inside, I saw that the walls of the room were spattered with blood from the squashed bodies of mosquitoes and vermin that tormented the twenty men day and night while they were imprisoned in that small room.

The prisoner stood up, and we had a few minutes of awkward conversation. As I was about to leave, I encouraged my Chinese Christian to say his prayers. The Chinaman fumbled in his pocket, took out his beads, and kissed the crucifix. In front of his fellow criminals and communist guards alike, he said, "I pray the Rosary continually."

The priest was very much impressed with the manifestation of this simple faith, and adds: "I don't know what the watching Communists thought of that man or of the people's courage in publicly showing their allegiance to the Rosary and to the Blessed Virgin. But I am sure they wondered, and perhaps they felt the stirrings of doubt about their power to destroy the faith they witnessed."

CHAPTER 44

QUEEN OF CONFESSORS

Three distinct meanings of the word Confessor are given, each deserving separate mention. In its primitive meaning the word is related to the original term of martyr or witness. Thus, those were confessors who had shown their willingness to die for their faith by bravely enduring imprisonment or torture, but were not put to death. The distinction is clearly drawn by the confessors of Lyons, who had suffered for their faith and were looked upon by their fellow-Christians as martyrs. While declining this title as of right belonging only to those who had actually died, they said: "They are already martyrs whom Christ has deemed worthy to be taken up in their confession, having sealed their testimony by their departure; but we are confessors mean and lowly." This clear distinction between martyrs and confessors is thus traceable to the latter part of the second century. Yet the name of martyr was retained, even during the third century, for persons still alive, as is evident from the writings of St. Cyprian, who gave the title to a number of bishops, priests, and laymen, condemned to penal servitude in the mines. Conversely, the title of confessor continued for many centuries to designate martyrs also, as the term confession, meaning a burial place of confessors and martyrs alike, would seem to imply.

After the middle of the fourth century the title appears in a more comprehensive sense. The word confessor then designates those who in virtue and knowledge exceeded others, and who by their writings, preachings, and holiness attracted the attention and veneration of their contemporaries. This recognition was continued after their death. Chapels were frequently erected in their honor, a distinction which in previous centuries had been the exclusive privilege of martyrs.

Since the time when the Roman Pontiffs reserved to themselves the right of beatification and canonization, the title of confessor has been conferred on those who were judged to have given evidence of heroic virtue, and whom God had approved by miracles. Because of their extraordinary, exemplary conduct, the confessors of the early ages were—as much as the martyrs—the pillars of the infant Church. By their outstanding virtue, their ardor, and spiritual energy, they were instrumental in spreading the tenets of religion among those who were interested in the new faith, while they did not fail to strengthen their weaker brethren. For them the Church had no other reason for its existence than to extend over the earth the Kingdom of Christ, and to render all men sharers in His saving redemption.

In this process of spreading Christ's Kingdom in a pagan world, it must have become increasingly evident to the first Christians, as it had grown on the apostles, that the Blessed Mother of our Lord could not be ignored. The Woman who in God's eternal plan, had brought Christianity into the world, could not be denied a place in the general scheme of salvation. Quite naturally the person of Mary remained somewhat in the background, at least during the first four centuries of the Church, but even during this period significant allusions to her exalted position, in particular to her share in the redemption, are by no means wanting. In the controversies of that period about the natures of Christ, the person of Our Lady came more and more to the foreground, until finally, in the fifth century Mary's true greatness was fully recognized, when the Council of Ephesus (431) summarily and without equivocation conferred her primary title of Mother of God. In this title all the other privileges of Our Lady are comprised, and a gradual development of her essential place in the economy of redemption was but a matter of time. While Mary's place in the spiritual life of Christians began thus to assert itself, there developed a holy emulation among ecclesiastical writers to give her the permanent position which she deserves, next to her Son.

If we look for a parallel of this growing zeal of the first Christians to arouse interest in Christ and Our Lady, we may perhaps point to the Legion of Mary, which has been so effective in our days in furthering the cause of Mother and Son. The Legion is young. It had its start in Ireland in the year 1921, but no single organization seems to have been so successful in reaching the vast multitudes as has been the Legion—even as the confessors of early Christianity. Working in small groups of ten to twenty members—each unit being called Praesidium, after a detachment of the Roman Legion which performed a special duty—the legion members go out in pairs to meet faithful and non-Catholics alike under the direct obedience and in true cooperation with the local pastors, in order to promote a spirit of good will and understanding in every home.

Their work is explicitly spiritual and eminently charitable, since the legionaries seem to be inspired by the words of Pius XI, who stated that, given five saints, he would convert any city. Given twenty-five saints, he would convert an entire country. They understand that anyone who wishes to enroll under the banner of Mary and work for our Lord, must begin with self-sanctification as an essential factor of success. On the other hand, the legionaries do not make the mistake of surmising that only those of advanced spiritual development and fair education can be attuned to the high ideals and the very detailed system proposed by the Legion. They rather start from the principle that the conversions of the early days of Christianity were wrought by the common people. Their approach, to be really effective, must be of an individual and intimate character, the appeal of one person to another person, according to the laws that rule the spiritual world, as Frederick Ozanam puts it: "The attraction of one soul is needed to elevate another." Here is no question of formal instruction, but of an effort of one heart to pour its supreme possession into another heart. For this reason there is no controversial spirit in true legionaries, nothing harsh, nothing overbearing. Every word breathes humility, affection, sincerity, in true imitation of their heavenly Mother whom they have taken as model.

It is no surprise that Satan fears the Legion at work, possibly because it is so closely allied to the spirit of the early Christians, who were confessors at heart and martyrs in aspiration. Turning once again to Red China, we find that bishops, priests, brothers, and sisters have been expelled from the country, because they were linked to the Legion. At one time twenty-seven Catholic young men and women of good families in Shanghai were banished to nameless prisons because they would not denounce the Legion. It is not difficult to understand why the organization-conscious Chinese Reds—drilled by the Russians not to care about individuals, but to seek out and destroy every concept and every piece of social machinery that could interfere with the completeness of the Communistic victory—are fighting the Legion. The Communists fear Our Lady, who is determined to conquer the world, as a potential menace. This fear is derived from the standard prayer of the Legion, in which the members implore Christ and His Blessed Mother to confer on them that fullness of faith in God and trust in Our Lady that will lead them to conquer the world. For this reason, the case against the Catholic Church has narrowed down in many instances to a direct attack on the Legion.

A relevant example is cited from the parish at Taai Wan. The legionaries were questioned about the activities of the

Legion over a period of fifteen months, day after day and long into the night. The security police forced them to turn over their rosaries, medals, and Legion prayer cards. They could not plead that their beads had been broken and discarded. They were made to hunt up the pieces and turn them in. They could not excuse themselves for having thrown away their prayer cards. Out they must go and find them. There was a demoniac frenzy to track down every and each handbook of the Legion in the diocese. The Reds had found out the exact number of books circulated, and each one had to be turned in. In like manner they went after the Legion standards and after any article used at the meetings of the legionaries. Here, they figured, was the hard core of the Catholic elite, who were likely to take Christianity under ground.

Perhaps we need more of this spirit of the early Christians, as exemplified in true legionaries. All of us are confessors at heart, and cherish the hope of converting others and leading them to God. Ours is a conviction of final victory for the cause of God; nor do we distrust our feeble efforts. For, we are in possession of a fundamental weapon which is like a double-edged sword, the sword of truth, of which Cardinal Newman writes: "I have an intense feeling in me as to the power and victoriousness of this truth. It has a blessing of God upon it. Satan can but retard its ascendancy; he cannot prevent it."

CHAPTER 45

QUEEN OF VIRGINS

Virginity is one of the covetable flowers of the Catholic Church. The virtue of purity is universal in its obligation, but virginal chastity belongs to that selected group of people in the Church who have answered the special counsel of our Lord, given to the few. Upon the suggestion of the disciples that in view of the many complications of married life it is not expedient to marry, our Lord answered: "Not all can accept this teaching; but those to whom it has been given. For there are eunuchs who were born so from the mother's womb; and there are eunuchs who were made so by men; and there are eunuchs who have made themselves so for the kingdom of heaven's sake. Let him accept it who can" (Matt. 19:11–12).

Virginity, then, suggests a reverence for bodily integrity, which is maintained for a supernatural motive. It is common to both sexes, although a physical, bodily integrity is discernible only in the case of women. Nor can virginity be lost against one's will, since a forced violation does not destroy it. The state of virginity, embraced for a higher motive, is generally accepted as the most perfect form of life, one which produces a special likeness to Christ and entitles the subject to a special reward, both in this life and hereafter. St. Thomas mentions such a particular reward in eternity, added to the essential happiness of heaven. This takes the form of an aureole, a special crown of bliss, granted to those who obtained one of three outstanding victories, in resemblance to Christ; either the victory over the flesh in virginity, the victory over the world in martyrdom, or the victory over the devil in the preaching of the truth. In his Apocalypse St. John makes special mention of virgins and describes their privilege before the throne of God: "And I saw, and behold, the Lamb was standing upon Mount Sion, and with Him a hundred and forty-four thousand having His name and the name of His Father written on their foreheads. And I heard a voice from heaven like a voice of many waters, and like a voice of loud thunder; and the voice that I heard was as of harpers playing on their harps. And they were singing as it were a new song before the throne, and before the four living creatures and the elders; and no one could learn the song except those hundred and forty-four thousand, who have been purchased from the earth. These are they who were not defiled with women; for they are virgins. These follow the Lamb wherever He goes" (Apoc. 14:1-4). In expounding Sacred Scripture exegetes explain this particular privilege, proper to Virgins, as their specific crown and added reward.

For centuries the Church sanctioned a detailed ceremony, found in the Roman Pontifical, by which virgins were dedicated to God. This followed closely on the rite of ordination, was reserved to the Bishop, and could not be repeated. When the general law of enclosure came into effect the ceremony was gradually omitted, but a vestige of it is still found in the solemn blessing of an abbess.

It is at once evident that Mary should bear the title of Queen of Virgins. The miraculous preservation of her bodily integrity is a dogma of the Catholic Church. God Himself prepared her to receive the Savior and become the Mother of God, while retaining her total integrity. In fact, hers was a threefold conception: in spirit, in soul, and in body, as John Tauler, the medieval mystic, indicates:

By her purity she pleased God well; by her humility she prepared Him a fitting dwelling place; by her love did she constrain God to descend into the depths of her spirit. This was the first generation of God in her spirit, which prepared a place all restful in the quiet detachment from created things. It is the eternal generation in Mary, comparable to the obscure night of the spirit wherein the darkness of the human intelligence received the dawning of the uncreated brightness. Where the divine light shines, no created light can remain, the created light of the spirit changing into the uncreated light of eternity. Thus it happened that Mary gave over her spirit into the uncreated being of God, and her soul sank away into the depths of humility.

Now she drew down into her soul the all-lovely sweet streams of the light of eternal wisdom; for as the Father brought forth His only begotten Son in her soul, He in turn new-formed her in Himself. From all eternity it was the will of the Father that His only begotten Son should assume human nature, and should be born of her in bodily form by the act of the Holy Spirit. But He needed her consent, and Mary was given to understand that she was chosen indeed for this high motherhood. Then she sank into deep self-abasement and understood that a common human being must not obstruct the eternal plans of God and, penetrated through and through with the divine majesty, and overcome by divine love, she was made willing to be the Mother of God. This is the second generation of Jesus in her soul.

At the same moment as she was thus absorbed in the Holy Spirit, the Angel Gabriel stood before her and greeted her, "Hail, full of grace, the Lord is with thee" (Luke 1:28). She was troubled at these words, both on account of her true humility, and because she was yet entranced in God. But when she spoke her *Fiat,* the power of God created the perfect body and members of Jesus. Then He created His pure and perfect soul, and joined body and soul together in Mary's womb. And instantly the Word was made flesh, and began to live among us. This is the third generation of God in the body of Mary, without any injury to her virginal integrity.

St. Augustine states that Our Lady was more blessed by the birth of our Lord in her spirit and soul, than by His birth in her body. This was confirmed by Jesus when He answered the woman of the Gospel, who praised His Mother: "Rather, blessed are they who hear the word of God and keep it" (Luke 11:28). It is because of this three-fold conception that Our Lady is the Queen of Virgins, and takes first place among those generous souls who, throughout the centuries, have imitated her and have dedicated their spirits and consecrated their souls to Christ in the complete immolation of their bodies. Virginal chastity is not the highest of virtues—the love of God being supreme —but there is no better means of acquiring the latter and bringing it to completion, than by embracing the state of perfection by the vow of chastity, according to the words of St. Paul: "The virgin thinks about the things of the Lord, that she may be holy in body and spirit" (I Cor. 7:34).

The same Illuminated Doctor, speaking to consecrated virgins, says:

Whoever would go very deep into God, must follow the example of Mary. Although we can never recompense God's great love for us, yet we should earnestly apply ourselves to Jesus, ourselves with all we are and all that we can do, as did His most beloved Mother, the Blessed Virgin, out of a heart most perfectly true to Him. Mary was wrapped into God and made one spirit with Him in the three powers of her soul. And she was all moved and guided by Him as a tool in the hand of a workman. She was poor in spirit. She was lifted up to God from a fathomless humility. She was self-annihilated, foregoing her own will, and without any longing except for God. And it was by reason of this state of her soul that God found an entrance to her in soul and body. I shall show you how we may rightly serve our Lord, helping you to become spiritually, as it were, our Savior's mother, God granting us the grace to generate and to bring forth His divine Son in our hearts. Mary was clean of spirit: for she did not cleave to any gifts of God, nor did she use them for her joy. She was clean of soul: she felt no attraction toward any created thing, but her soul was adorned with all virtues. She was clean of heart and pure of body: she was never moved to sin, being like the shining angels of heaven. She was an interior spirit: her sweet affectionate yearnings were all upward toward God, and the outgushing waves of the divine love poured down from the Holy Trinity into her soul. She was deeply recollected: all the powers of her soul were constantly employed in God's praises. She was a faithful heart: her heart was inflamed with love's fiery longings to be lost in the incomprehensible abyss, which is God.

Thus did she find her Beloved. She had penetrated the sovereign majesty with her sweetness; she had wounded the eternal wisdom with her comeliness; she had drawn the eternal goodness with her love. She did not live her own self, but she lived only Him who is the life of all the living. All her beginning and ending, all her doing and not-doing was in God. For she was ever united to God, never turning away from Him and His holy presence for a single instant. No creature left any impression on her soul or ever entered there, for like the angels she saw all things singly in God. Him alone did she find in her soul's depth, in the essence, in the innermost recesses of her spirit. Hence, she was never turned outward, looking for high things and multiplicity; she was ever poor, clean, interior, God-like, more a creature of heaven than of earth.*

No soul can ever attain to such purity, but, be it ever so far in its resemblance, the virginal chastity of every dedicated virgin on earth must follow this pattern.

CHAPTER 46

QUEEN OF ALL SAINTS

The preceding invocations designated Mary as Queen of individual saintly groups. This one marks her as Queen of All Saints. It is a well-known doctrine of the Catholic Church that the degree of glory of the saints in heaven corresponds to the degree of grace and charity which was theirs at the moment that they departed this life. For that reason we must say that Mary's present glory, which overshadows the glory of angels and saints alike, was essentially hers before her entry into heaven. But the question is this: Was Our Lady's initial grace higher than the final grace of all the angels and saints taken together? If this can be proved, Mary's superior status today is plain by a fortiori evidence.

When we once again recall the words of Pius IX, we have, before all else, an argument from authority in favor of this proposition. "From the beginning," Pope Pius states, "and before all ages, God selected and prepared for His only Son the Mother from whom He would be born in the blessed fullness of time. He loved her by herself more than all creatures . . . that is why, drawing from the treasures of His divinity, He endowed her, more than all the angels and saints, with such an abundance of heavenly gifts that, all beautiful and perfect, she appeared in such a plentitude of innocence and holiness, that, except God's, no greater than hers can be conceived." The significance of the passage is plain, and the words allow only one explanation. Because of His singular predilection for His future Mother, God placed Mary before all creatures, angels and saints alike, both taken individually as well as collectively.

To this argument from authority theologians add two others, which may be called theological conclusions. The first is based on the words of St. Thomas, who claims that Mary's initial grace was given to her in order to prepare her to be a worthy mother of the Savior. The strength of the argument lies in the efficacy of grace, which is given to all with regard to the beatific vision as its final reason and purpose. But Mary's grace was given for the twofold purpose of preparing her for heaven, and thus to qualify her to become the Mother of God. The latter measure of grace must have been proportionate, at least remotely, to the divine maternity, which itself is a grace of surpassng nature inasmuch as it pertains to the hypostatic order.

The second argument traces back to the uncreated love of God for the Blessed Virgin. Since grace is the effect of the active love of God, and is proportionate to it, we must conclude that the more a person is loved by God, the more superabundant are the graces which he receives. These are the words of St. Thomas: "God loves one more than another by the fact that He wills him a greater good." Now there is no greater good among created grace than to be selected to become the Mother of God. God loves the angels as highly privileged creatures, next to men whom He loves as His adopted children; but Mary alone He loves as His Mother. Consequently, the grace bestowed on Our Lady from the beginning, in proportion to this love, must have surpassed the measure of grace given to all others together. This, besides making Mary God's most beloved creature, establishes her as Queen of all, since her selection was in relation to all, and above all in time and eternity.

Next to this universal queenship of Mary in the court of heaven, is her supremacy among the saints on earth. Here we take the word "saint" in the biblical sense. A common term in the Old Testament to designate those who belong to God, the word "saint" was applied in the New Testament to those who believed in Christ. Frequently used by St. Paul, and found in the Acts of the Apostles, those are saints who are separated from other men, are attached to Christ, and are sanctified by the indwelling of the Holy Spirit. All these claim Our Lady as their Mother and Queen. The saints on earth are strengthened and sanctified by the graces which pass through her hands, and she does not cease to intercede for them before the throne of God. St. Alphonsus says: "The eternal Father made Jesus Christ the King of justice, and Mary the Queen of mercy." To this argument, based on Mary's universal mediation, St. Albert the Great applies the history of Queen Esther, who herself was a type of our heavenly Queen.

In the fourth chapter of the Book of Esther we read that, in the reign of Assuerus a decree was issued which condemned all Jews to death. Mardochai addressed himself to Esther in order to have her interpose with Assuerus, obtain the revocation of the decree, and thus save her people from extinction. Esther declined, fearing that a request might irritate the King beyond measure. But Mardochai insisted that she must remember her patent obligation; that God had placed her on the throne to save His people. The Queen yielded and went to see the King. Assuerus was moved with generosity when he saw Esther standing before him, and inquired after her desire. The Queen answered, and said: "If

I have found favor in thy sight, O King, and if it pleases thee, give me my life for which I ask, and my people for which I request" (Esther 7:3).

The application is obvious. Mary approaches our Lord to plead, not for herself, but for her people. Well does she know that she has found favor in the eyes of God, for she is not only the Queen of God's people, she is also the Mother of the Son of God. To this St. Alphonsus adds: "Mary is under an infinite obligation to the Son for having chosen her to be His Mother; but it cannot be denied that the Son is under obligation to her for having given Him His humanity. Jesus, therefore, to pay as it were what He owes her, and glorifying in her glory, honors Mary in a special manner by listening to, and granting all her petitions."

In a revelation to St. Bridget Our Lady said: "I am the Queen of heaven, and the Mother of mercy. I am the joy of the just, and the door through which sinners are brought to God." Mary takes pride in her particular privilege to plead for them who are placed in her trust. Saints as well as sinners are her concern, for they are all her people, but the latter enjoy priority, and, for each soul saved by her help a new jewel is added to her crown in eternity.

CHAPTER 47

QUEEN CONCEIVED WITHOUT ORIGINAL SIN

Mary's initial fullness of grace, of which we spoke in the preceding chapter, presents two separate aspects. A positive

side, which concerns her absolute pure and holy conception; and a negative side, which treats of her miraculous
preservation from all sin. Both aspects have entered in our
discussion before, but the latter deserves a more detailed
examination because of the glorious doctrine contained in
the present title.

Following are the words of Pius IX, which established
the dogma of the Immaculate Conception:

"We declare, announce, and define, that the doctrine
which states that the Blessed Virgin Mary, in the first instant
of her conception, by a singular grace and privilege of God
Omnipotent, and because of the merits of Jesus Christ the
Savior of the human race, was preserved free from all stain
of original sin, is revealed by God and must therefore be
believed firmly and with constancy by all the faithful."

Taking the words of the solemn document as a foundation, we find three salient points to be considered. First, that
the Blessed Virgin Mary was preserved free from all stain
of original sin, in the first instant of her conception. This
was the main point of controversy since the twelfth century.
Before that time, and even during the heated debate of
scholastic theology, no one questioned the fact of some special privilege which was accorded to Mary in the form of an
anticipated sanctification, at least similar to the privilege
granted to St. John the Baptist, who was sanctified in the
womb of his mother. The question was whether Mary's
sanctification was *merely* an anticipated one, such as St.
John's, or whether this privilege was extended to an earlier
moment. In other words: was Our Lady, like other humans,
freed from the stain of original sin already contracted, or
was she free from that stain entirely by virtue of a special
privilege? The difficulty was emphasized by the words of
St. Paul, who seems to rule out any distinction, "as all have

sinned and have need of the glory of God" (Rom. 3:23). Repeatedly the Apostle emphasizes this need of a Redeemer for all men without exception. The reasoning was obvious. If Mary did not contract original sin at all, she would not have been redeemed. Conversely, since she was redeemed, she must have contracted original sin. Duns Scotus was the first theologian to reach a solution of the problem, when he indicated that what was subsequent in the order of nature could be simultaneous in point of time. Speculatively, the soul must be created before it can be infused and sanctified; in reality, the soul of Mary could be created and sanctified at the very moment of its infusion into the body. This would constitute for Our Lady a preservative redemption—which is indeed a redemption, and of a much higher status than a liberative redemption, since it is better to prevent than to cure. The Bull *Ineffabilis* ended all controversy by stating definitely that Mary was preserved from all stain of sin, from the first moment of her conception.

The second point of the solemn declaration of Pius IX deals with this privilege as bestowed upon Mary through the merits of Jesus Christ, by a singular grace and privilege of God omnipotent. The idea of this singular redemption brings to mind that Mary, as a child of Adam and proceeding from him by natural generation, would have incurred the hereditary taint, had not God decided from all eternity to preserve Our Lady by an unmatched privilege because of her Son. Here the merits of Christ were applied by anticipation, in the manner in which all the elect had shared in our Lord's merits before His Incarnation. At the same time we are reminded that Mary possessed this particular privilege in a way different from her Son. Jesus was not redeemed by the merits of another, not even by His own. He needed no redemption, since His conception was virginal and due to the operation of the Holy Spirit of God, so that our Lord did not descend from Adam by way of natural generation, and thus He was exempted peremptorily from the hereditary consequences of Adam's fall.

The third point considers the doctrine of the Immaculate Conception as revealed by God. As such, it must be contained, at least implicitly, in the deposit of revelation, that is to say, in Holy Scripture and Tradition. Holy Scripture makes no direct or categorical statement about this glorious privilege of Our Lady. There are, however, two sacred texts which figure prominently in confirming the doctrine at hand. First, the scriptural passage which contains the promise of the redemption, and which mentions the Mother of the Redeemer. "I will put enmities between thee and the woman, between thy seed and her seed: she shall crush thy head and thou shalt lie in wait of her heel" (Gen. 3:15). The Vulgate text, from which the English translation is taken, represents the woman as the one who crushes Satan's head. The Hebrew text, at least the present-day one, by a change of pronouns indicates not the woman, but the seed of the woman as the conqueror of the serpent. There is, however, no essential difficulty, since the enmity against the serpent is represented as common to both, and thus the victory must be common to both in their essential unity of Mother and Son.

Since these words of the protogospel in themselves offer no conclusive proof of the Immaculate Conception, Pius IX turns to the Fathers of the Church as to the living voice of Tradition. Summarizing this voice, he explains: "With the words, 'I will put enmities between thee and the woman, and thy seed and her seed,' God in His very first announcement to the world gave the sovereign remedy His divine mercy had prepared for the renewal of the human race. He therefore repressed the audacity of the deceiver, the devil, and wonderfully lifted up the hope of mankind. The Fathers teach us that this divine announcement clearly and distinctly points to the merciful Redeemer of the human race in the person of the only-begotten Son of God, Jesus Christ, and designates the Most Blessed Virgin as His Mother. It expresses notably the bitter enmities of both against the devil. Wherefore Christ, the mediator between God and man, upon assuming our human nature, erases the handwriting of the decree which was against us, and fastens it as conqueror to the Cross. Also, bound to Him by the closest and most indissoluble bond, the Most Holy Virgin carries into effect, together with Him and by Him, the perpetual enmities against the poisonous serpent, is completely victorious over it, and crushes it by her immaculate foot."

The same document quotes the words of the Archangel, "Hail, full of grace, the Lord is with thee. Blessed art thou among women" (Luke 1:28), as well as the corresponding salutation of Elizabeth (Luke 1:42). The Holy Father does not claim conclusive authority for these words, for which reason he again turns to the Fathers. These, with great uniformity, give the traditional exegesis and explain the passage to contain a direct reference to Mary's total exemption from all sin, and every stain of sin, both actual and original. Thus enlightened by the allusions of Holy Scripture and Sacred Tradition, and inspired by the Holy Spirit, Pius IX made his final pronouncement, and stated that the doctrine of the Immaculate Conception was a divinely revealed dogma and was to be accepted as such firmly and with constancy by all the faithful.

The theological proof of the doctrine at hand is an elaboration on the words of St. Thomas who claims it to be reasonable that she who gave birth to the Only-begotten of the Father received greater privileges of grace than all others. Thus the Angelic Doctor who, in the argument about the Immaculate Conception, leaned to the negative side of the question, furnished the very principles along which the true solution of the problem was drawn. Along with the Thomistic argumentation in its proper development, Pius IX states that, just as the Word proceeds eternally from a most holy Father, it was becoming that He should be born in time from a most holy Mother, to whom the splendor of sanctity had never been lacking. In order that Mary should be able to repair the effects of Eve's fall, overcome the wiles of the devil, and give supernatural life to all in Jesus Christ, it was eminently becoming that she herself had never been in a fallen condition, a slave to sin and the devil. It can by no means be said that Our Lady sinned in Adam. Rather was she created as daughter of Adam, because she was destined to be the Mother of the Redeemer. Thus her bodily relation to Adam was from the beginning entirely subservient to her bodily relation to Christ. This being the case, it could never be admitted that our Lord would have allowed His Mother to be, even for one instant, under the power of His archenemy.

When Pius IX by his solemn proclamation on December 8, 1854, established the dogma of the Immaculate Conception, he merely reiterated the almost universal sentiment of the Catholic faithful, which for centuries had celebrated the feast of the Immaculate Mother on that date. Nearly a century before the solemn announcement of the dogma, the Immaculate Conception was declared principal Patron of all the possessions of the crown of Spain, including those in America; and the first council of Baltimore in the year 1846 elected Mary, under this title, as the principal Patron of the

United States, a decision which the Holy Father confirmed on Feb. 7, 1847.

The insertion of this invocation in the litany of Loreto was originally granted by Pius IX to the Bishop of Mechlin in 1846, and, after the definition of the dogma, the Congregation of Rites by various rescripts authorized additional dioceses to make a similar addition, until the insertion became universal.

CHAPTER 48

QUEEN ASSUMED INTO HEAVEN

The dogma of Mary's glorious Assumption is a corollary of the dogma of the Immaculate Conception. It was solemnly declared to be contained in the deposit of Christian faith by Pope Pius XII on Nov. 1, 1950. Because of the perfect harmony of graces with which God favored His Blessed Mother, it is only natural that, once He had given her the privilege of being conceived without original sin, the privilege of her bodily Assumption into heaven after her death should follow as a necessary consequence.

Mary's bodily death is a mystery in itself, and cannot be explained by the general law of death to which every human being is subject. For death, in final instance, is a punishment which follows original sin, as God clearly explained when He forbade man to eat of the tree of knowledge of good and evil. "For in what day soever thou shalt eat of it, thou shalt die the death" (Gen. 2:17). Death is inevitable only in so far as man has no supernatural claim to the eternal continuation of his nature. Adam and Eve forfeited this supernatural claim both for themselves and their posterity; but the punishment was not extended to the Blessed Mother inasmuch as she remained totally free from original sin. The penal debt, although it was binding on the rest of mankind, was never placed upon Mary, as the Council of Trent defines (Sessio V, 5).

The fact remains that Mary did die, according to the constant and general belief of the Church. This can be explained only through analogy with the example of our Lord. The death of Jesus was freely accepted in expiation of the sins of mankind. Our Lady's death, although lacking this expiatory character, was also voluntarily accepted, lest by her exemption the Mother should appear greater than the Son. But her death was neither painful nor sorrowful. It rather came in the form of a dissolution resulting from the supernatural power of divine love which separated the soul from the body and speeded her on her way into the arms of God. The sacrifice made under the Cross in greatest mental agony whereby our Mother shared in the sufferings of Christ's death, was thereby outwardly completed in a sweet and loving manner which resembled a slumber rather than a violent death.

Mary's departure, being neither an expiatory death nor a death of punishment, belongs entirely to the order of grace. This is still more emphasized by the fact that her body did not fall prey to the natural consequences of death. It escaped the fate of corruption, which has been especially designated by God as the penalty of sin: "For dust thou art, and into dust thou shalt return" (Gen. 3:19). Death is not dishonorable. In the mind of the Christian it is a question of victory rather than of defeat. In final instance, it signifies a conquest of spirit over matter. But the decomposition which follows death does not share in this glorious possibility which death offers. It is and remains a punishment and, even in the case of the just, appears as a remnant of the curse of sin. For this reason it was entirely excluded from the body of Christ and Our Blessed Lady, who were not subject to sin nor to its punishments, and the words of the Psalmist, "nor wilt Thou give Thy Holy One to see corruption" (Ps. 15:10), are not to be understood exclusively of our Lord, but must of necessity be extended to His Mother.

From the doctrine of Mary's exemption from the dominion of death and its consequence, the corruptibility of the body, it is only a step to her privilege of immediate resurrection. If a separation of body and soul had lasted longer than the purpose of death required in the economy of redemption, that separation would just as well have signified a dominion of death, as would the decomposition of the body. The honor of the Mother required a complete safeguarding of her entire existence, and the material service performed by Our Lady, whereby she used the substance of her body for the formation and sustenance of Jesus, demands the glorification of her body in a distinctive manner. Mary's singular, intimate, and absolute union with Christ in His sufferings and death requires a perfect participation with Him in His life of glory. Both as instrument and cooperator in the work of redemption, Mary must most perfectly experience in herself the fruits of that sublime work. So much the more since only in a risen and glorified body could she, in union with Christ, effectively continue her office of mediatrix, and be the perfect surety of the efficacy of the act of redemption for the rest of mankind.

As Pope Pius XII aptly remarked in his apostolic constitution which established the dogma of the Assumption, in Mary are fulfilled the words of the Psalmist: "Arise, O Lord, into Thy resting place: Thou and the Ark, which Thou hast sanctified" (Ps. 131:8). The Fathers have considered the Ark of the Covenant, built of incorruptible material and placed in the Lord's Temple, as a type of the most pure body of the Virgin Mary. The vision of St. John, where he beheld the same Ark of the Covenant in heaven (Apoc. 11:19), and saw Our Lady preserved and exempted from the corruption of the tomb and raised to transcendent glory, confirms the final and entire fulfillment of this figure.

There still is a second argument, which is not less cogent. It is found in that most intimate association of the Mother of God with her Son in His redeeming passion. The argument, proceeding from two revealed premises, leads to a theological conclusion which is also implicitly revealed. It may be formulated as follows: Christ's victory over Satan was complete, since it included victory over sin and death, and found its crowning glory in the Resurrection and His Ascension into heaven. But Mary, the Mother of God, was most intimately associated with Jesus on Calvary in His victory over Satan. Hence she was also associated with Him in His victory over death by her anticipated resurrection and her Assumption. This was the main argument advanced by the Fathers of the Vatican Council, when they requested an early and dogmatic definition of the doctrine of the Assumption. It was founded on the text of Genesis, which had also formed the foundation of the dogma of the Immaculate Conception. The victory over Satan and sin was, according to God's plan, a combined victory of Jesus and Mary. But a complete victory over sin must include a victory over death, since the latter is a consequence of sin.

It could perhaps be objected that it would be enough were Our Lady associated with her Son's victory over death by her final resurrection on the last day. But this would not

be a complete victory, since perfect victory over death includes exemption from bodily corruption, and demands an
anticipated resurrection and assumption into heaven. As we
read in the Collect of the Mass of the Assumption: "She died,
but she could not be retained captive by the bonds of
death." Only after the mortal body has put on immortality
is final victory over death completed. St. Paul says: "This
corruptible body must put on incorruption, and this mortal
body must put on immortality. But when this mortal body
puts on immortality, then shall come to pass the word that
is written, 'Death is swallowed up in victory' " (I Cor.
15:54).

The Holy Father states the particular reason why he defined the dogma at this specific time: "It is in order to stir
up the faithful to a stronger piety toward their heavenly
Mother. . . . Thus, while the illusory teachings of materialism and the corruption of morals that follows from
these teachings threaten to extinguish the light of virtue
and to ruin the lives of men by exciting discord among
them, in this magnificent way all may see clearly to what a
lofty goal our bodies and souls are destined."

CHAPTER 49

QUEEN OF THE MOST HOLY ROSARY

For centuries the Rosary has been the privileged prayer
of Catholics. Although it is addressed to the Blessed Lady,
it is chiefly a praise and thanksgiving to the Son. Adapted
to every state of mind, it offers to God a song of perpetual

homage for the divine mercy shown to His Mother. When Mary prayed her *Magnificat,* and said: "Henceforth all generations shall call me blessed" (Luke 1:48), she could have hardly anticipated to what extent that prophecy would be fulfilled. Ever since the veneration of the Mother of God began to take shape in apostolic times, the faithful have repeated the Angelical Salutation as a reminder of Mary's glorious participation in the work of the redemption. The gathering of these prayers into a garland of roses, which we call the Rosary, is only an expression of the untiring efforts of her children to perpetuate devotion to our Blessed Lady. Father Lacordaire says: "Love has but few words to utter; and, while it is ever repeating these words, it never repeats itself."

Without going into the disputed question of the origin of the Rosary, we may say that the use of prayer beads to count identical prayers dates back to time immemorial. In the Christian world the use of paternosters is centuries old. As the word clearly indicates, these appliances were originally used to count Our Fathers. In the twelfth century the Hail Mary, as a formula of prayer, came into use, and, in the course of the same century, the custom of reciting 50 or 150 *Ave Marias* became a common practice. No doubt the same method was employed to count the Hail Marys, and the common rosary beads, as we know them today, are still designated by the name "paternosters" in several European countries.

The fifteenth century gave a great impetus to the general practice of reciting the Rosary by the establishment of Rosary confraternities under Dominican auspices. An acceptance of a more uniform system in its recitation is without doubt to be ascribed to the tireless effort of the Dominican Fathers, for which reason the Rosary in the Western Church is properly named the Dominican Rosary. In 1571 a special feast in honor of Our Lady of Victory was instituted by St. Pius V for the first Sunday of October, in commemoration and gratitude for the naval victory of Lepanto gained by Don Juan of Austria over the Turkish fleet. This victory was largely ascribed to the special protection of Our Blessed Lady, since it corresponded wonderfully with the processions made at Rome that same day by the members of the Rosary confraternity. Two years later, upon request of the Dominican Order, Gregory XIII changed the name of this feast to that of the Holy Rosary, and permitted the commemoration to be kept in all churches which possessed an altar dedicated to the Holy Rosary. The observance was extended by Clement X, in 1671, to the whole of Spain, and in 1716, upon another important victory gained over the Turks in Hungary, Clement XI ordered the feast to be observed by the universal Church. Benedict XIII first gave the feast a set of proper lessons in the second nocturn, while Leo XIII raised the observance to the rank of a double of the second class, and added the present invocation to the Litany of Loreto (1883). The celebration of the feast is now kept on the date of the Battle of Lepanto, October 7th, except by the Dominicans who still observe the original first Sunday of October.

The Rosary considers the three great mysteries of salvation: the incarnation, the redemption, and the life beyond the grave. It places before us, in concrete form, the life of our Lord, who came down from the Father and who returned to Him after His life's work was completed. It contains the whole of Christian dogma in all its splendor and elevation, like a true book of morality and spirituality which is presented to us in the combined example of Jesus and Mary. It is a very practical form of prayer since the mysteries of the Rosary are designed to be reproduced in the life of every Christian. For, in our progress toward God there are likewise three stages. The first one, that of knowledge, is represented by the joyful mysteries, which contain the good news of the incarnation and open to us the way to salvation. The second stage is the one of effort and labor. It indicates our way, which is often painful to nature, but which is ever shaped after our Lord's own example. The final stage is that of rest in the possession of eternal life. The Rosary is a true introduction to even the highest forms of prayer, one of intimate converse with Jesus and Mary. It has been called a school of contemplation, and for many saints it has proved to be just that. To them it is more than a devotion, more than a formula of prayer; it is a form of life, one which leads them through the several stages of purification to the most desirable union with God.

No Christian is too simple or unlettered to make use of the Rosary, and, while it has been for some the vehicle of high contemplation, for others it has been the unmistakable means to lift them above the sordid interests of life and to preserve their faith in all simplicity. A striking example of the latter is reported to us by a Spanish missionary, who recently discovered a lost Catholic community on a far-away island of the Pacific, where the people, with the help of the Rosary, had kept the faith for 150 years, without benefit of clergy.

This remote island is off the northern coast of Luzon in the Philippines, and is known as Bayabon Claro. It has been a legendary island of mystery ever since shipwrecked sailors found asylum there centuries ago. In 1680 a Spanish missionary, Father Mateo Gonzalez, transferred the inhabitants to other areas, and the island remained deserted until 1800, when a second shipwrecked group found refuge there.

The Dominican Father, Florentine Castanon, reached the island on July 27th, 1952, in an eight-ton boat, after ten hours of struggle with strong currents and stormy weather. He said he had a most grateful surprise when he found, not semi-savages, but a group of good and humble people who were overjoyed when they learned he was a Catholic priest.

The inhabitants numbered 233: 117 men and 116 women. Only two could read and write, but they knew how to baptize and had their own little chapel dedicated to St. Dionysius of Athens, first century bishop and martyr. The people still remembered the hierarchical system of the Church, and knew that the Pope—*U tadi no apo Dios*—was Christ's vicar on earth. Father Castanon relates:

"The people wanted to spend hours and days with me to learn doctrine and prayers. Their great-great-grandfathers had known how to recite the Rosary in Spanish. However, being isolated for 150 years, they had forgotten the ten joyful and sorrowful mysteries, and only remembered the five glorious mysteries, which they recited on Sundays.

"Their practice of reciting the Rosary kept these people united to the Faith of their fathers, while the only other prayer they knew in common was the Litany of the Saints in Latin. One of the old men had been charged with performing baptisms, and used the correct form."

The Dominican Missionary remained on the island 62 days. He blessed 35 marriages, administered 56 baptisms, and confessed and gave Holy Communion to 172 persons. He returned home on a Philippine naval vessel which was sent to pick him up, not without assuring the people who had come to the shore to bid him farewell, that he would return to the lonely island.

There is little we need to add to this striking example which so gloriously illustrates the power of the Rosary. As it remained the consolation of these simple people, and retained their faith intact for over 150 years, so it must be our tower of strength in a world that cannot retain the faith without the help of Mary and her Rosary.

CHAPTER 50

QUEEN OF PEACE

This invocation was inserted into the Litany by Benedict XV, during World War I. The title is Mary's by divine right, since, as the Mother of the Savior, she gave to the world the One who was announced as the "Prince of Peace" (Is. 9:6).

Peace is the one objective all people of good will desire. It may be defined as "tranquillity of order," which cannot be established or maintained without God. We wish to believe in humanity; but our trust has been severely shaken by the recklessness of nations, and by the disregard they show for the rights and justified claims of others. When peoples substitute selfishness for charity, and greed for justice, instead of making God our last end, who can be simultaneously possessed by all, they reap the ugly fruit of their perversion. The instability of our world affairs, and the inability to adjust them satisfactorily, offer undeniable proof that universal world peace cannot succeed, unless the rights and claims of the Author of peace and order are taken into account. There is no substitute for God; exterior peace cannot be obtained unless nations return to God, and the reign of Christ is re-established in the kingdom of Christ.

For this return of straying souls to God, we must have re-course to Mary's intercession, who is the universal Media-trix and Mother of all men. It has been said of sinners, who seem forever lost, that they must be confided to Our Lady. The same holds for nations who have gone astray. Our Lady's concern is not confined to individuals. It embraces entire nations, who ought to live beneath the life-giving rays of the Gospel and experience the saving influence of the Church.

After Pius XII dedicated the world to the Immaculate Heart of Mary in a general way in 1942, he repeated the consecration on July 7, 1952, explicitly for Russia. Well did he recognize with his predecessor, Pius XI, that the two great evils of the age are to be found in materialistic and atheistic communism on the one hand, and in unrestrained nationalism on the other. Both evils are found combined in the aims of the rulers of the Kremlin, and only a radical return to faith and religion can bring about a much desired change. Such a miraculous change is not beyond human hope. Our Blessed Lady herself suggested the possibility during her apparitions at Fatima, when she requested world prayers and penance for the conversion of this great country, and demanded that Russia be dedicated to her. Pius XI had already ordered special prayers for the conversion of Russia, when he ordained that the Leonine prayers, which are said after each low Mass, should be offered henceforth for this specific intention. Pius XII willingly confirmed and re-newed this regulation, "since," he said, "the religious situa-tion is not improved, and we are animated by the same most ardent affection and concern for the peoples of Russia."

Even today Russia is very much the country of Our Blessed Lady. Nowhere do people display such childlike and tender confidence in the help of Mary. For obvious reasons this vivid devotion has gone underground and is forced to remain hidden. But it will not stay there forever. Russia's *Bogoroditza,* "She who gave birth to God," will not desert her beloved people. As Pius XII expresses it: "The hope of salvation can never be absent wherever hearts are turned with sincere and ardent piety to the most holy Mother of God. Though attempts be made by men, no matter how powerful and impious, to root out from the minds of the citizenry holy religion and Christian virtue, and though Satan himself may strive with every means at his command to foster this sacrilegious struggle—as is described in the words of the Apostle of the Gentiles, 'For our wrestling is not against flesh and blood, but against the Principalities and the Powers, against the world-rulers of this darkness, against the spiritual forces of wickedness on high' (Eph. 6:12)—yet, when Mary interposes her powerful protection, the gates of hell cannot prevail."

The salvation of this beautiful country of Russia, as well as of the entire world, will not be accomplished unless we unite in prayer. Our Lady alone can align classes and peoples which are ranged against one another in fundamental dissensions. Nor is there anything more effective to save a nation from total disaster than a formal dedication to Mary by the entire country, particularly when the consecration is performed by the common Father of the faithful, the supreme Pastor of souls.

The Holy Father recalls that there are many among the Russian people who still preserve their Christian faith within the innermost sanctuary of their consciences, and who suffer in silence for the restoration of their country to Christian ideas and ideals. It is our duty to help them by our co-consecration in a common cause. We must share in their sufferings, since we share in their merits. Their present hour of affliction is not to last forever, as Our Lady promised: "In the end my Immaculate Heart will triumph, and an era of peace will be conceded to humanity." Other persecutions throughout the centuries have afflicted the Church and have passed away. They left her better and stronger. Thus the Church goes from struggle to struggle, and from victory to victory, as our Lord said to the disciples of Emmaus on the evening of His Resurrection: "Did not the Christ have to suffer these things before entering into His glory?" (Luke 24:26)